Playful Activities

for

POWERFUL
PRESENTATIONS

Playful
Activities

for

POWERFUL
PRESENTATIONS

Bruce Williamson

 **Whole Person Associates Inc**
Duluth, Minnesota

Library of Congress Cataloging in Publication Number: 93-60577
ISBN: 0-938586-77-7

REPRODUCTION POLICY

Unless otherwise noted, your purchase of this volume entitles you to reproduce a modest quantity of the worksheets that appear in this book for your education/ training activities (up to 100 copies per year). For this worksheet reproduction no special additional permission is needed. However, the following statement, in total, must appear on all copies that you reproduce.

Specific prior written permission is required from the publisher for any reproduction of a complete exercise with trainer instructions, or large-scale (more than 100 copies per year) reproduction of worksheets, or inclusion of material in another publication. Licensing or royalty arrangement requests for this usage must be submitted in writing and approved prior to any such use.

For further information please write for our Permissions Guidelines and Standard Permissions Form. Permission requests must be submitted at least 30 days in advance of your scheduled printing or reproduction.

Printed in the United States of America by Versa Press

10 9 8 7 6 5 4 3 2 1

WHOLE PERSON ASSOCIATES INC
210 West Michigan
Duluth MN 55802-1908
218-727-0500

*Thanks to everyone who has helped me
grow lighter in spirit and younger at heart*

ACKNOWLEDGMENTS

Many friends, colleagues, and clients have encouraged and nurtured my work, especially during those early days of learning and growing as a presenter. I would particularly like to acknowledge J. Sig Paulson, Rob and Clair Pennington, Tobin Quereau, Tom Zimmerman, Shay Tindall, Tim Ramsey, Robin Pinckard, Lydia Pendley, Jaynee Fontecchio, Patty Sheehan, Kay Davis, Richard Imprescia, Linda Newcomb, Bob Czimbal, and Maggie Zadikov.

Special thanks to Don Tubesing, Susan Gustafson, Patrick Gross, and everyone else at Whole Person Associates for helping bring the dream of this book into reality.

Some of the activities in this book have been adapted and developed from those experienced at conferences and workshops, learned from various books, and discovered in conversation with friends. These sources include Matt Weinstein and Joel Goodman (*Instant Recess, When You Were Little, May We Have This Dance?*); Robin Pinckard (*Sweet Somethings*); Shay Tindall (*Raccoon Hands, When You're Up*); Tim Ramsey (*Getting to Know Us*); Bob Czimbal (*Leaf Pile, Food Groups*); Roger von Oech (*What's the Point?*); and Karl Rohnke (*Hoopla, Sock It to Me*).

CONTENTS

LAUGHING FOR THE HEALTH OF IT

WONDERING AROUND

TAKING IT HOME

An Age Ago

Like most small wild things
you're hard to track, but
this field's full of paths
worn smooth by your feet running
to hidden places I once knew,
when I belonged to your tribe.
In that distant age I too was
known as a swift child of the hills.

Bruce Williamson

INTRODUCTION

You're never too old for recess.

Bruce Williamson

THE PURPOSE OF THIS BOOK

Playful Activities for Powerful Presentations helps facilitators and group leaders create dynamic and healthy "playgrounds" where participants can freely and safely explore, rediscover, and experience the power of play.

The activities presented here are designed to serve as a kind of "cookbook of play." Each "recipe" is structured in the same way to make it easy to follow. Try out a few recipes as they are written to see how they work for you. Find out which activities become your favorites. Feel free to add new ingredients and variations, or invent whole new activities. But most of all, use these creative activities to spice up your presentations and make them more powerful and fun.

BEING A CHILDLIKE GROWN-UP

Like Pooh Bear in *The House at Pooh Corner*, I often go out for "a fast Thinking Walk by myself," and sometimes these walks take me past a neighborhood elementary school during the recess period. Usually I stop at the fence for a moment, listening with amazement to the shouts and screams and laughter, and watching happiness radiate out in all directions from that playground. On those days it's easy to feel right down to my toes the boundless energy, exuberance, and enthusiasm of these young humans who have been let outside to play for a while.

Many of us, however, have lost touch with these valuable childlike qualities and become disinterested, rigid, and even cynical. We lock away our child selves and abandon them for a variety of understandable reasons, ranging from personal traumas we experienced as children to cultural messages we believe as adults. We often talk to ourselves in a negative "real adult" voice, saying that it's wrong to act silly or laugh and play too much. With all that static it's hard for us to hear the voice or feel the persistent tug of the small child selves within us who want (and need) our adult selves to just take a break from working so much, go outside, and learn how to play.

When we deny our childlike natures, we reflect a still widely-held societal belief that play is "children's work," optional and frivolous, "not real," and something people are allowed to do only after all their work is done.

These myths and beliefs (though well-entrenched) are being proven false. People are discovering that if they regularly take time to play they are better able to stay well-balanced, happy, resilient, optimistic, healthy, creative, and more effective and productive—especially in the workplace.

People who did not have happy childhoods—who for various reasons never really got to be children—can begin enjoying *now* what makes so many children's lives special and magical. Adults can learn to appreciate the lifelong value of having a more childlike approach to living, and become what I call "childlike grown-ups."

Child*like* is very much different from child*ish*. Childlike grown-ups are free to choose the best of both worlds. They are different in every way from childish adults, who have never grown up.

Becoming a childlike grown-up is an art, an attitude, and for many people an entirely new kind of behavior that will increase the joy, energy, and creative power in their lives.

PLAY'S THE THING

Seen in the past as mostly the realm of children, play in its many healthy forms is now being regarded as another important, powerful, and positive tool people can use to keep themselves in proper balance. In his book *Positive Addiction,* William Glasser talks about fun as a human need—a species requirement in the same category as air, food, water, and shelter, another form of nourishment essential for healthy, happy, and productive lives. What does play do for people?

Increases happiness. During play some people shed so much pain, worry, and fear that it looks as if a plastic surgeon had worked on their faces. Play helps break up destructive patterns and old routines, and encourages more joyous approaches to living.

Relieves tension and stress. Playing and having fun offer people a highly effective stress management tool, particularly because they so often stimulate the use of that beneficial, high-potency drug called laughter.

Fosters learning and creativity. Most people were told from an early age that they could go out and play *only* when all of their work (whatever kind) was done. The real facts about the value of play are much closer to the words of a five-year-old girl who one day clearly let her mother know, "When I play, it gets me smart for my homework."

Enhances bonds with real children. The more we develop our childlike nature as grown-ups, the greater ability we have to be with and be trusted by real children in our lives. Children are drawn like magnets to grown-ups who know how to play and who like to play.

Reactivates the sense of wonder. The sense of wonder is one of the great master keys to lifelong happiness, learning, and creativity. Most of the greatest artists, inventors, and creators in all cultures have been people who could maintain their childlike sense of wonder, their continual delight in the world, and their enthusiasm for living.

Improves communication with others. Playful activities help stimulate healthy interaction between people in all kinds of personal and professional settings. Positive experiences of communication, cooperation, trust, healthy touch, teamwork, group bonding, and personal sharing almost always tend to increase and improve as people play together.

Even a few playful activities at the beginning of any conference, workshop, or other program can help participants overcome nervousness, participate more fully, and communicate more easily with each other.

HELPING ADULTS LEARN TO PLAY

> No one can play a game alone. One cannot be human
> by oneself. There is no selfhood where there is no
> community. We do not relate to others as the person
> we are; we are who we are in relating to others.
>
> **James P. Carse,** *Finite and Infinite Games*

TIPS FOR FACILITATORS

How can we expect to help adults learn how to play if we haven't
worked through our own barriers to being more playful? Our
own playfulness shows in everything we do with a group, and
more than anything else demonstrates how a childlike
grown-up acts.

Become more playful yourself. To develop your childlike
nature, learn some playful skill you've always wanted to master but
didn't think you could learn, such as performing magic tricks,
riding a unicycle, juggling, or whatever. Learning this new skill
will help you understand what your participants go through when
you ask *them* to be more playful. You benefit because you stretch
the limits of your own playfulness. When you share with your
groups your own frustrations and breakthroughs in learning this
skill they will benefit because they'll know you have experienced
what it feels like to take a risk in being more playful.

Lure people into play. Because so many people have so many
barriers and reasons for resisting play, become a "Pied Piper of
Play" and make the idea of playing as irresistible as possible. The
activities in this book lure people into play by using a "structured

spontaneity" approach, which means they set certain boundaries, guidelines, and suggested "rules" (hopefully not rigid ones) within which participants can then be as free and creative as possible. Few grown-ups really feel comfortable (or even safe) with completely unstructured activities, especially when they are just beginning to figure out how to be more playful in their lives.

Know when to play and when to observe. As facilitators and group leaders we are naturally inclined to be helpful to others, or we wouldn't be in this line of work. One of the hardest lessons we must learn is to step back and let people do the activities without hovering over them and hoping they will have the insights and experiences we want them to have. As the writer Wendell Berry says, "Put it in their reach, not in their lap."

Whenever possible involve yourself in the action. Each of us needs to experience what it is we are trying to evoke in our groups.

Your primary responsibility, however, lies in effectively facilitating the activities. Before you can join in, you need to ensure that participants feel safe and are interacting and playing together.

Grow with each workshop. Part of the fun of play workshops is the spontaneity of what happens with each group. No person or group of people ever plays with an activity exactly the same as another. Our carefully planned outlines must often be set aside in order to deal with other realities that surface in the workshop. And, of course, Murphy's Law occasionally rules the day.

When something doesn't go as well as you planned, rather than berate yourself with negative self-talk simply say to yourself, "Next time." "Next time here's how I'll introduce that activity. Next time I plan to take more time at this point in the workshop," and so on.

The beauty of this approach is that it focuses the mind on a process of constant improvement. It allows us to honor the fact that we have done the best we could at any moment, and also know that the next time we can do even better. This process can really help us grow as facilitators and keep us much less rigid about everything having to be done a certain "right" way.

Write down new ideas. Make notes about the new and different ways groups play together and the amazing ideas and insights they share with you and each other. People often tell inspiring stories and suggest resources you will want to remember. Find an effective way to keep track of these comments and observations, but avoid taking notes in any way that diverts your attention away from the group or distracts the group during an activity.

Encourage people to reflect and write. At certain points in the workshop allow a few minutes for people to quietly write about what they are experiencing. Writing also serves as a creative way for introverted people to take an often necessary break from the more energetic, expressive activities.

Know when silence really can be golden. Whenever you sense group members hesitating to share, wait a full *thirty seconds* longer before you say anything to move the discussion along. You may be surprised how often some of the best communication begins to happen at exactly the point when you want to break in and get things moving.

Whenever possible, encourage group sharing before you as the facilitator contribute your own thoughts.

Ask the group to help. During the workshop have participants open boxes, unpack the parachute, pass out materials and supplies, and so on. Kids love to help!

Deal with people's fears, issues, and concerns. Over the years a few people have told me how terrified they felt right before coming to a workshop. Some people have even sat out in their cars debating about whether or not to come inside. At the beginning of some workshops you may want to tell participants that many people often feel nervous, scared, or even terrified about the thought of being asked to play. Participants need to know that others have and are feeling this way, and that the play itself will quickly allow them to let go of their fears. As the facilitator you must try to honor, understand, and deal effectively with these fears whenever you can.

Although the activities in this book can be highly therapeutic in people's lives, *do not* offer them as a substitute for professional counseling and therapy.

Ask for feedback. At the end of a workshop ask people to take about five minutes and write you a letter. Tell them that they are free to share with you anything they wish about the workshop and their experience of playing. They can sign the letter or not.

Many of these letters will be "keepers" you can pull out from time to time as wonderful sources for personal inspiration and professional insight. In them, people will let you know, often in very personal ways, what kind of impact the workshop has had in their lives. These letters will also provide you with great ideas for constantly improving your program.

In addition to the feedback letter, you may want to ask participants to fill out a simple workshop evaluation form of your own design. Here are four important questions to ask:

1. What was the most important or significant thing you learned at the workshop?
2. What specific actions are you planning to take in your life as a result?
3. What suggestions do you have for changing or improving the workshop the next time it is offered?
4. What other resources about laughter or play do you recommend?

If participants have no objections, tape recording your workshop also provides a useful way for learning more about the content and style of your presentations.

COMMUNICATING PLAYGROUND "RULES"

In any workshop lasting over an hour or two it is helpful if participants have a sense of what the playground "rules" are, especially the ones most important to you. I've found it works best to ask the group to come up with the guidelines they want to follow as they play together. What invariably happens is that they list at least 75 percent of the items I wanted to share. With that kind of group ownership it's then easy to suggest adding the few remaining ones from my list. Here are some of the guidelines I feel are most important.

Participation is optional. When I lead activities I always hope as many people as possible will *want* to play, but sometimes people sit out. They may simply be tired or feel uncomfortable with too much touch, or have any other of a dozen good reasons why they aren't participating. Sometimes deep feelings have been triggered that need some reflection time alone. If I can help these people or support them in some way I will, but I won't attempt to push them out of their seats and onto the playground. Participation is always optional, and I respect people's wishes not to play.

"Play hard, play fair, nobody hurt" is the original motto of the New Games Foundation, a pioneering group of inventors, teachers, and facilitators of cooperative play. Their six-word guideline needs no explanation.

Agree on attention-getting signal. Play workshops are by definition, like children, *supposed to be* noisy, rowdy, and rambunctious. You will find it helpful at the beginning of a workshop to have the whole group agree on some friendly way for you to get their attention when necessary, such as raising one hand in the air. When participants see you raise your hand, for example, they raise their hands in the air, stop what they are doing, and become quiet.

An Audubon bird whistle, a kid's slider whistle, a Nature Company "energy chime," a Whole Person Associates wooden "train whistle," and several other children's noise makers are excellent physical attention-getting devices. These tools also add a whimsical and playful touch to the process of getting people's attention.

For the kinds of activities contained in this book, however, it is *never* appropriate to blow a traditional "coach's whistle" to get the group's attention. Many people associate a variety of unpleasant experiences with that piercing and familiar sound, including strict rules, coaches yelling, and kids getting sucked into highly competitive (but not very playful) team sports. This kind of whistle cannot aid you in helping adults learn how to really play—*unless* you want to use it to help participants remember what they thought and felt when they heard that sound as children.

It's OK to make up new rules. The "rules" for each activity are suggestions and guidelines about what usually works. But occasionally an activity may not work as well with one group as it does with others. Part of the playfulness in any workshop is for the facilitator and the group to know it's OK to make up some new (or fewer) rules and try them out.

Respect the privacy of others. Outside the workshop people are always free to talk specifically about what *they* experienced but only generally about the behaviors of others.

Agree on photo opportunities. In many cases photographs or even a videotape can become a wonderful reminder and souvenir of a grown-up playground experience. Whenever possible, however, have pictures taken by a photographer who is also an active participant in the group. Try making group pictures a kind of playful activity in itself. At the very least, make sure you have cleared the taking of any pictures with the whole group ahead of time; don't assume it is all right with every person there. Many people coming to play may already feel self-conscious, and the presence of a photographer may have an even more inhibiting effect.

CHOOSING PARTNERS AND FORMING GROUPS

Many people experience a degree of fear bordering on panic when asked to "go find a partner" in the midst of a bunch of strangers. Part of our job as facilitators is to help make that process as nonthreatening as possible.

Twoing. To ensure that people feel safe and keep having fun, use a simple "twoing" activity to get them creatively arranged in various combinations. (I am indebted to the writer Zenna Henderson for coining the word "twoing" in one of her novels.)

Twoing helps participants playfully form pairs of "play buddies," small groups of four to six "kids on the block," and large groups, or "playgrounds," of twenty or more people. Twoing activities are fun and effective because they have absolutely no relation at all to how or why someone "normally" picks partners. For example, you might ask participants to think of exotic favors of ice cream, a vegetable they hated as children, or their favorite tree. Then have them find one or more people who also like that flavor or tree, or hated that same vegetable. You can have people think of their favorite animal, and then have those who like giraffes, for instance, pair up with those who like mice. Or take a different approach and have people find others with the same shoe size—tell them they're looking for their "sole mates." The sillier and more bizarre the combinations the better. Ask participants for suggestions.

At the end of the twoing process you will almost always have some solitary flavors (or trees or animals, etc.) wandering around still looking for partners, so tell them it's OK to link up with anyone else remaining at this point. Make sure they don't feel left out.

Twoing is also a great method for picking who goes first in groups or pairings. For example, in an activity involving pairs have participants figure out which partner likes chocolate ice cream and which one likes strawberry. Then you choose which flavor goes first. This simple twoing exercise can also help you with other activities later on. If you need to gather people in two large groups, for instance, you can have all the chocolate lovers from the earlier activity gather in one group and all the strawberry lovers in another. Or if people have already paired up for a few activities and you need them to form small groups of four to six "kids on the block" you can have them stay together in pairs and just go link up with other pairs. Likewise, a group of six kids on the block can join with several other groups to form a "playground" of between twenty-four to thirty people.

People will often form strong bonds with each other in even a short time using these different groupings. At conferences even days after a play workshop, people still run into their partners and playground buddies with a wonderful sense of recognition, connection, and delight.

Twoing activities make the process of blending and bonding a useful, funny, and playful experience. When people get caught up in the whole frenzied business of finding others who meet the same silly criteria, they forget about feeling nervous and scared. Once participants successfully make that first contact with a stranger it usually becomes much easier from then on for even shyer people to interact with others.

DETAILS, DETAILS, DETAILS

Although the activities in this book are designed to be used with little preparation, your workshops or presentations are not. The activities will be less effective if you haven't dealt with the following details before beginning your program.

Group size. To generate enough group energy for extended periods of play, you'll need a minimum of ten to fifteen people. If you have the personal desire, a large enough play area, a superb sound system, and enough trained helpers, you can have hundreds of people—even a thousand or more—playing together at one time.

Physical challenges. Not all of these activities work quite as well for people who have various physical problems and challenges. With a little ingenuity, however, they can easily be adapted to meet these people's special needs. Discuss ideas with the affected persons, and when appropriate, ask the whole group to suggest ways to make each activity as inclusive as possible.

Dress code. Whenever possible, advise participants ahead of time to wear comfortable clothing. As a male facilitator conducting these playful activities, I have never felt that ties were appropriate garb for anyone. If I ever *need* to wear one, though, I plan to buy a colorful Crayola® crayon tie I once saw displayed at an arts and crafts fair.

Workshop location. Whenever possible make sure there are no other classes being held on *any* side of your workshop room. This is especially important in hotels where large ballrooms are often partitioned off to create smaller classrooms. Since your workshop is designed to stimulate such noisy activities as laughing, playing, singing, frolicking, and dancing—you *will* end up disturbing other quieter groups around you. Participants and speakers in those other rooms can become quite upset at the sometimes dramatic distraction from their own programs, and if this happens, no one wins.

Estimating room size. When estimating the proper room size for play activities, (1) get a figure for the number of people you expect to attend the workshop, (2) estimate the amount of space you would need if that expected number of people were seated classroom-style at a "normal" lecture-style presentation, then (3) multiply that estimated space by a minimum factor of three times.

Always double-check with conference and hotel planners to make sure they understand that your workshop really does need three times the "normal" space, and that this extra space is actually provided. It's difficult and frustrating for people—including the facilitator—to try and play in a room that is much too small for the activities you have planned. Square rooms generally work much better than long, narrow ones.

Chair and room arrangement. Most people expect classroom-style seating when they walk into a conference or workshop room. If your room is arranged like that, you can involve the group in their first playful activity by saying, "When I say go, clear all the chairs out of the center of the room as fast as you can." On the other hand, if you set up a different—even peculiar—chair and room arrangement, participants will immediately know your workshop is different.

Avoid using podiums, which separate you from participants. Instead, request enough six-foot-long tables to hold all of your notes, tapes, toys, materials, and supplies.

Presentation materials. When working with audio-visual devices, keep in mind that less is more. Use technology to enhance your presentations when needed, but avoid depending on it. Make sure you have back-up bulbs and batteries handy for the inevitable (and always badly-timed) snafus.

- *Microphone:* For workshops in which you need a microphone, a dependable wireless mike is almost always the best choice. It allows you the freedom to move quickly and creatively around the room. With very large groups, however, make sure participants can actually see you above the crowd, or you'll find people looking at the loudspeakers whenever you're talking.

- *Cassette player:* For clarity and convenience in playing music with large groups it is usually best to have the cassette player connected directly to the room's sound system.
- *Overhead projector:* Generally more versatile than slide projectors, use them to project worksheets, pertinent cartoons, and inspirational quotations.
- *Flipcharts:* For standard flipcharts use water-basc markers whenever possible because they are nontoxic and don't smell or bleed through the paper. Stick to solid colors that can be read easily from a distance.

PLAY CAN MAKE A DIFFERENCE

Early one morning after a huge storm a child walked along a beach. In every direction she looked she saw starfish—thousands, perhaps hundreds of thousands, of starfish washed up on the sand. The child then noticed a man also walking along the beach, engaged in a curious activity. He would bend down, pick up a starfish, walk into the water, and gently toss it back into the ocean. Then he walked back, picked up another starfish, and repeated the process. The child walked over to the man and asked what he was doing. He told her the starfish would all die if they didn't get back into the water soon. "But there are so many starfish!" the child exclaimed, looking up and down the cluttered beach. "It won't make any difference what you do." The man was quiet for a moment, and then said, "It makes a difference to this one," as he picked up another starfish and threw it back into the sea.

Play can and will make a positive difference to "this one and this one and this one"—to each one of those people who come to your workshops and discover there, with your help, that life really is ". . . much too important to be taken seriously."

There is as much difference between us and ourselves as between us and others.

Michel de Montaigne

GETTING TO KNOW US

1 BACK TO NURTURE BINGO (p 4)

Using a special Bingo card, participants fill in answers to imaginative and thought-provoking questions about humor, laughter, and play, and then go around the room sharing their insights with others. (10–15 minutes)

2 GETTING TO KNOW US (p 7)

People use words and physical movements to loosen up and playfully learn the names of all the other people in their small group. (5–10 minutes)

3 HAND DANCING (p 10)

With music playing in the background, individuals take turns in pairs gently initiating and following each other's physical movements. (5–10 minutes)

4 MINGLE (p 12)

Participants pretend to be shy people and repeatedly shuffle around the room murmuring a special word until they bump into and enthusiastically greet many other people. (4–5 minutes)

5 NAME TAGS (p 15)

Using materials familiar to all kindergartners, participants create colorful "nonstandard" name tags to wear during the workshop. (5–10 minutes)

6 RUSH HOUR (p 17)

In this playful exploration of trust issues, individuals take turns being "cars" and "drivers" and steer each other around a crowded highway (room). (5–8 minutes)

7 SOMETHING WONDERFUL (p 20)

Using the basic kindergarten show-and-tell format, small groups of participants share physical objects that have some marvelous quality, special significance, or magical meaning to them. (10–15 minutes)

1 BACK TO NURTURE BINGO

Using a special Bingo card, participants fill in answers to imaginative and thought-provoking questions about humor, laughter, and play, and then go around the room sharing their insights with others.

GOAL

To learn more about each other by sharing interesting thoughts and experiences.

GROUP SIZE

Unlimited

TIME FRAME

10–15 minutes

MATERIALS NEEDED

One **Back to Nurture Bingo Card** for each person. (Whenever possible, print the cards on white or light-colored index cardstock.)

PROCESS

1) Give the following instructions:

➤ Take a few minutes to fill out as many boxes on your **Bingo Card** as you like. Write on the back of the card if you need more room.

➤ When you have completed at least five boxes, find one other person and share one of your answers with that person.

➤ After you have shared your answer with this other person, have him or her sign that particular box on your **Bingo Card.**

© 1993 Whole Person Associates   210 W Michigan   Duluth MN 55802-1908 (218) 727-0500

Sign your own box whenever you complete one of the activities (the boxes with the dotted lines inside).

➤ Repeat this process with different people until you've shared all your answers.

➤ Whenever you have five squares in any direction (including the free space in the middle) signed by different people, yell out "OGNIB" (BINGO said backwards) as loudly as you can.

➤ Remember, the way to "win" in this game of Bingo is to have lots of fun meeting and learning neat stuff about other people in the group.

VARIATIONS

- Have participants share their answers in small groups of 5–6 people as a way to get to know each other better.

- Have small groups of 5–6 people fill out the **Bingo Card** together, with each person answering two or three questions. Then have each group find another small group, exchange answers, and perform the activities with each other.

NOTES

- I am always impressed at the unlimited, amazing range of interesting thoughts and answers the **Bingo Card** provokes. It provides an excellent way for strangers to get to know each other quickly.

© 1993 Whole Person Associates   210 W Michigan   Duluth MN 55802-1908   (218) 727-0500

BACK TO NURTURE BINGO

What is one of the funniest movies you ever saw?	What are two of your favorite cartoon strips? Why?	If you could travel in time, when and where would you go?	⌐ ¬ HOP ON ONE LEG OR SKIP AROUND THE ROOM FOR AT LEAST ONE MINUTE ⌐ ¬	Who was a favorite grown-up when you were young? Why?
What was your favorite story as a child? Why did you like it so much?	What would you do if you had a magic wand?	Name someone who makes you laugh. What is it about that person that cracks you up?	What was (or is) a favorite childhood toy of yours?	⌐ ¬ EXCHANGE A HUG WITH THREE OTHER PEOPLE
List three foods that children like.	Name something you would like to see invented.		What fills you with a sense of wonder?	If you could live anywhere, where would you live?
⌐ ¬ LAUGH OUT LOUD FOR 45 SECONDS WITHOUT STOPPING ⌐ ¬	What was your favorite Crayola® crayon color when you were little?	What kind of store would you like to open?	Describe a perfect day.	Children like to
If you could be any animal, what would you be? Why?	⌐ ¬ SING A CHILDREN'S SONG WITH TWO OTHER PEOPLE	Children are	What music do you find most relaxing? Most energizing?	Something that makes you smile is

DIRECTIONS   Fill out as many boxes on this **Bingo Card** as you like. When you have completed at least five boxes, find another person and share one of your answers with that person. After you have shared your answer with this other person, have him or her initial that box on your **Bingo Card**. Initial your own box whenever you complete an activity (the boxes with the dotted lines inside). Then go find a different person and repeat the process of sharing an answer. Whenever you have five squares in any direction initialed by different people, loudly yell out "OGNIB" (BINGO said backwards).

2 GETTING TO KNOW US

People use words and physical movements to loosen up and playfully learn the names of all the other people in their small group.

GOALS

To establish playful contact with others in a small group.

To reinforce the process of learning people's names and getting to know them better.

GROUP SIZE

Unlimited, in small groups of 8–10 people

TIME FRAME

5–10 minutes

MATERIALS NEEDED

None

PROCESS

1) Have participants form small circles of 8–10 people.

2) Tell participants that you are going to share with them a very special way to easily learn the names of all the other people in their little group, an almost magical method of getting to know each other.

3) Have each group choose someone to go first.

4) Tell participants to silently think of their first name and then the first letter in their first name. Have them then silently think of a positive, playful, or childlike word that begins with the same first letter as their first name. For example, a person named Bill,

which begins with a *B,* might choose "Boisterous" or "Bashful" or "Bubbly." Someone named Mary might choose "Mighty" or "Mischievous" and so on.

5) Tell participants to silently create a two-word name that combines their first name with that other word beginning with the first letter of their first name. In this way, Bill might become "Bubbly Bill" or "Bill Bashful." It doesn't matter which of the two words comes first.

6) Next, have participants silently think of a distinctive movement or gesture that somehow expresses their new name. For example, Bill could pantomime blowing bubbles as a movement to express "Bubbly Bill."

7) After everyone has thought of a name, have the people who are going first step into the center of their circles, say their two-word name, make their special movement, then step back into the outer circle.

8) Standing where they are, everyone else in the circle immediately repeats that first person's two-word name and his or her movement, performing a kind of "instant replay" of what that person just said and did.

9) This process continues with the next person to the left or right of the first person. However, after this second person steps back into the circle and everyone else repeats his or her two-word name and movement, they then *also* repeat the first person's name and movement before moving on to the third person.

10) From then on, every time a new person says his or her name and performs a movement, everyone else repeats *that* person's name and movement as well as the names and movements of all those who have gone before.

11) Tell groups who finish the activity early to talk quietly together about what it was like getting to know each other.

VARIATIONS

- To limber up a group, have participants choose a stretching or bending motion that they can insert into the repetitive sequence described above.

- Instead of a movement, have people choose a sound to go along with their two-word name.

NOTES

- This activity serves as a wonderful icebreaker with most groups. Although some people panic a bit at the thought of learning all these other names, by the end of the activity they are usually surprised at how well they have learned them. The repetitive speaking and moving really do work.

- Fewer than eight people per group will not provide much of a challenge for the participants.

3 HAND DANCING

With music playing in the background, individuals take turns in pairs gently initiating and following each other's physical movements.

GOALS

To experience the power and pleasure of moving in rhythm to different types of music.

To have an opportunity to closely observe and follow the movements of another person.

GROUP SIZE

Unlimited, in pairs

TIME FRAME

5–10 minutes

MATERIALS NEEDED

Cassette tape player and a variety of relaxing and highly energizing music.

PROCESS

1) Have participants face each other in pairs, standing about two feet apart. Tell them to position their hands upright and at shoulder height with their palms facing forward and about an inch apart from the other person's palms. One person starts off as the Hand Dancer, the other person is the Mirror. Roles will be reversed later in the activity.

2) Start the music and tell the hand dancers to move their hands and bodies in rhythm to the music while keeping their feet rooted in one place. Tell the mirrors to simply reflect and follow all of the hand dancers' movements.

3) After a minute, signal the participants to reverse roles.

4) After each person has played both roles, switch to a different energy and tempo of music, and repeat the process.

VARIATIONS

- Allow the hand dancers and mirrors to move their feet so that they can travel around the room together.

- Have participants use face movements only, including various forms of smiling and laughing.

- Delete the music and have people mirror the sounds the other is making. You could have them combine this with the physical movements as well.

- Have three people team up, assigning two mirrors to one hand dancer.

NOTES

- The activity is about communication and teamwork, about the need to let go of what we want to do and allow another person to lead us. This activity is not about trying to competitively fake out a partner by moving really fast.

RESOURCES

Exercise your imagination in choosing the variety of music. I happen to favor a cross between soothing classical music and John Phillip Sousa marches.

© 1993 Whole Person Associates   210 W Michigan   Duluth MN 55802-1908 (218) 727-0500

4   MINGLE

Participants pretend to be shy people and repeatedly shuffle around the room murmuring a special word until they bump into and enthusiastically greet many other people.

GOAL

To meet each other in a playful, nonthreatening way.

GROUP SIZE

Unlimited

TIME FRAME

4–5 minutes

MATERIALS NEEDED

None

PROCESS

1) Have people gather together in a "clump," a loosely disorganized group, facing the center of the play area.

2) Ask how many people sometimes feel shy when they are in a group. Be sure to raise your own hand!

3) Tell participants that you have an activity guaranteed to help them meet some other friendly people in the group they don't know yet.

4) Give the following instructions:

➤ Assume the postures and attitudes of shy people, such as downcast eyes, hands wringing together, and so on.

➤ When I give the signal to begin, everyone shuffle forward in the shy person mode toward the center of the group, chanting the following magic word, "Mingle, mingle, mingle."

➤ As you bump into each other, suddenly and miraculously you will no longer be shy. Take a moment to greet each other the way children often greet new playmates, without barriers or preconceptions, just saying "Hi!" to one another and perhaps learning the other person's name.

➤ After you greet another person, immediately go back into the shy person mode, shuffling forward and chanting "mingle," until you have bumped into at least seven or eight other people in this way.

VARIATIONS

• Have participants ask each person they meet the same question. For example, "What's your favorite color (animal, car, vacation spot, season, etc.)?"

• As people are shuffling forward, ask them to find other people based on something they share in common. For example, "Mingle around until you bump into someone wearing an article of clothing the same color as something you're wearing." Or, "Mingle around until you find at least one other person with about the same size feet as yours."

Remember, as people are mingling and trying to find those other people, they are shuffling forward in shy person position, looking down at the floor and at other people's legs and feet. Only when they find that other person will they then look up and say "Hi!"

NOTES

• When I lead this activity I sometimes like to quote the "ad" for "Powdermilk Biscuits" that ran on Garrison Keillor's original

---

Prairie Home Companion radio show, that biscuit mix that "gives shy people the courage to get up and do what needs to be done."

• One thing I like about this activity is that it reminds me of my own shyness when I'm not up on stage as the presenter or facilitator, with microphone in hand and flipchart and markers at my side. This activity can help participants acknowledge that they may feel a little bit uncomfortable not knowing other people, yet want to make new friends.

© 1993 Whole Person Associates   210 W Michigan   Duluth MN 55802-1908 (218) 727-0500

5 NAME TAGS

Using materials familiar to all kindergartners, participants create colorful "nonstandard" name tags to wear during the workshop.

GOAL

To create a name tag that playfully and colorfully expresses the child in people.

GROUP SIZE

Unlimited

TIME FRAME

5–10 minutes

MATERIALS NEEDED

Blank white index cards (the 3 x 5 inch or 4 x 6 inch sizes work well); single hole punch; brightly colored yarn; scissors; crayons and watercolor markers in various colors; self-esteem and other child-type stickers (available at school supply stores, card shops, and discount stores).

PROCESS

1) Prepare some of the materials before the workshop starts by punching holes in two corners of each index card and precutting three-foot lengths of different-colored yarns. (By tying a piece of yarn through the holes in the card the name tag can be worn looped around a person's neck.) Make up your own name tag ahead of time.

2) As people come into the workshop, or as one of the first activities, have them spend a few minutes using the available materials to create their own unique name tags.

3) Make sure you have enough materials, supplies, and working space to go around.

VARIATIONS

• After people have gotten to know each other, have half the group exchange name tags with each other while the other half of the group closes their eyes as the switch is made. That half of the group then opens their eyes and goes around putting the right name tags around the right necks. Then reverse the process.

• Have people use the normal white self-adhesive name tags but encourage them to go out of their way in making the tags more colorful and expressive.

NOTES

• Most workshop name tags are pretty boring. "Hi, my name is _____." The name tags created in this activity, however, help produce a much more visually playful environment. People usually smile when they look around the room and see those wonderfully decorated names hung around people's necks.

• The cards-on-yarn name tag is great for when you don't want people to know each other's name during a particular activity. You can simply have participants flip their tags over.

6 RUSH HOUR

In this playful exploration of trust issues, individuals take turns being "cars" and "drivers" and steer each other around a crowded highway (room).

GOAL

To have an experience of trusting another person in an exciting and playfully supportive environment.

GROUP SIZE

Unlimited, in pairs

TIME FRAME

5–8 minutes

MATERIALS NEEDED

Attention-getting devices such as whistles, sirens, chimes, etc. One large black-and-white-checkered flag (optional). Three large green, yellow, and red cloth flags (or large colored cardboard circles) to use as traffic light signals (optional). Sticks for flags (optional).

PROCESS

1) Have the group form pairs using a nonthreatening "twoing" activity.

2) Give the following instructions:

➤ To begin, decide which person in your pair will be the "driver" and which person the "car." It doesn't matter what role you choose now because you'll reverse them later on.

➤ Cars, tell your drivers what type of vehicle you would like to be, then face forward in any direction you wish and cross your arms over your chest with your elbows (bumpers) pointing out.

➤ Drivers, stand behind your car and place your hands (steering wheel) on your car's shoulders.

➤ The purpose of this activity is for the drivers to guide their cars safely around the room (highway) without having any accidents.

➤ Cars, you may find this activity more exciting if you close your eyes and make car noises as you are being driven around the room.

➤ After a minute or so you'll reverse roles and the drivers will have their turn at being cars.

3) Tell the drivers to first make sure their seatbelts are fastened and then start their engines. If you have a checkered flag, wave it as the starting signal. Otherwise, just say "Go!"

4) Allow the car and driver team 1–2 minutes to drive around together.

5) If you have traffic light signals, use them to occasionally and silently control the movement of the drivers. Otherwise, just let the cars and drivers speed around the room.

6) When the time is up, blow a whistle, yell "Stop!" or wave a red-light flag or card.

7) Have the cars open their eyes and become drivers and the drivers close their eyes and become cars.

8) At the end of this second round of driving, allow some time for participants to share their experiences and feelings with each other. This is best done between the car and driver pairs, or by having two or three pairs team up together to share.

© 1993 Whole Person Associates   210 W Michigan   Duluth MN 55802-1908 (218) 727-0500

VARIATIONS

- If you use this activity with teenagers, you may want to title it "Driver's Ed."

- Not everyone may want to participate, and sometimes the group can't be divided evenly into pairs. In these cases let the "leftover people" choose alternate roles if they want. You might ask someone to handle the traffic light signals. You could add an extra person to driver/car teams as a "back-seat driver." Extra persons could also serve as highway patrol, pulling speeders over to the side of the room (highway), complete with siren sound effects.

- In a large gym—or ideally a track with running lanes—you could play this activity as a kind of stock-car race, although taking special care to keep it just for fun and deemphasizing competition.

NOTES

- Some people will not want to close their eyes, and that is always all right. But closing the eyes intensifies the experience (and the fun!) of letting go and trusting the other person.

- Be ready to intervene or completely stop the activity if a driver seems to be deliberately trying to run his or her car into others.

- With some groups, this activity could be used as a playful way to set up other activities centered on such issues as self-esteem and goal-setting.

- Some "trust" activities—though stimulating and powerful— don't usually get people laughing during the instructions. This one does.

© 1993 Whole Person Associates   210 W Michigan   Duluth MN 55802-1908 (218)727-0500

7 SOMETHING WONDERFUL

Using the basic kindergarten show-and-tell format, small groups of participants share physical objects that have some marvelous quality, special significance, or magical meaning to them.

GOALS

To share some special, precious, or wonderful physical object with other group members.

To rekindle a personal sense of wonder.

GROUP SIZE

5–6 people per group

TIME FRAME

10–15 minutes

MATERIALS NEEDED

None (See **Notes**)

PROCESS

1) You will need to contact participants ahead of time and tell them to bring "something wonderful" with them to the workshop. (Use those exact words and see what happens.)

2) During the workshop, have people sit in small circles and, just like in kindergarten show-and-tell, share and talk about the wonderful things they brought with them. (If objects are not too fragile or priceless, encourage people to pass them around the circle.)

NOTES

- This is one of the quickest, most enjoyable, and magical ways I know for a group of people to really get to know one another. The amazing diversity of physical objects brought in to share with the group and what is said about those items reveal many special, wonderful facets of the people who are sharing.

- You may want to have your own small box of wonders available for people who forgot to bring something or who came to the workshop at the last minute.

© 1993 Whole Person Associates   210 W Michigan   Duluth MN 55802-1908 (218)727-0500

It takes a very long time to become young.

Pablo Picasso

TOUCHING THE CHILD WITHIN

8 CHILD'S GARDEN (p 24)

In this guided meditation, participants are asked to visualize in great detail a peaceful, beautiful garden where they meet and play with their own inner child. (10–15 minutes)

9 CHILDREN R 2 (p 29)

With the help of a special card deck, participants reflect on the qualities they most admire in children and then go around introducing themselves to each other *as* those childlike qualities. (10–15 minutes)

10 FOOD GROUPS (p 40)

Small groups are asked to list foods they think belong to the four "kid" food groups and, on some occasions, to actually sample some of these "kid" foods. (10 minutes)

11 SWEET SOMETHINGS (p 44)

Each participant has an opportunity to repeatedly hear a variety of positive messages that reinforce, nurture, and affirm the specialness and preciousness of his or her child spirit. (15–20 minutes)

12 THAT'S MY KID! (p 48)

Participants focus on pictures of themselves as small children to affirm the beauty and playfulness of their inner child. (10–15 minutes)

13 WHEN YOU WERE LITTLE (p 50)

Participants share with partners at least one positive memory of something they did to play and have fun when they were kids. (10–15 minutes)

8 CHILD'S GARDEN

In this guided meditation, participants are asked to visualize in great detail a peaceful, beautiful garden where they meet and play with their own inner child.

GOALS

To create an imaginary place that can be visited regularly to honor, nurture, and play with the inner child.

To come up with positive images of what it means and what it feels like to be a childlike grown-up.

GROUP SIZE

Unlimited

TIME FRAME

10–15 minutes

MATERIALS NEEDED

None

PROCESS

1) Use the following words—or your own words—to guide the group on an exploration of a very special "garden."

   Let's all get as quiet and comfortable as we can. When you feel ready, simply close your eyes . . . Now slowly take in a breath, hold it for a moment, and then release it fully . . . Take another deep breath, slowly in, and slowly out. And now another.

Each time you breathe out relax more deeply. Each time you breathe out feel all the tension and stress draining right out of your body. You don't have to be anywhere else except right here, right now. You are taking care of you and that feels good.

With your eyes still closed, begin to imagine a very special garden—your garden. Begin to paint a picture of what that garden looks and feels like.

Now simply say to yourself, "I am in my garden now!" and instantly you are in your garden, sitting comfortably in your favorite chair. Just sit quietly for a few moments in that really comfortable chair you love, the one that fits you so well.

As you sit there in your garden, you notice that all of your senses are absolutely fully awake. The sun is warm on your skin. The clouds are so puffy and white they look as if they've been painted onto the perfectly blue sky. It's a day when every single cell in your body is saying "Thank You!" and "Yes!" just for feeling so alive.

Look around your garden right now. What do you see? What kind of trees, plants, flowers, and vegetables are growing there?

Take a really deep breath. What do you smell in your garden? What kinds of flowers and trees are blooming today?

Take off your shoes and socks. Wiggle your toes. Let your feet touch the ground of your garden. What do you feel underneath your bare feet?

Right behind you is a fruit tree, one of your favorites. And you've come to your garden at just the right time, because the fruit is perfectly ripe. All you have to do is stand up and pick it. Take a bite. How does it taste?

Begin walking around your garden while you're eating that piece of fruit. Birds are singing everywhere. They seem to be welcoming you back to your garden. Are there any other animals around?

Up ahead you see a child skipping along, stopping every few yards to look at something up in a tree or on the ground. You call out to the child, who hears you and stops skipping as you come closer. The child looks at you very quietly, almost solemnly.

Suddenly the child smiles at you, with the biggest, most radiant smile you've ever seen, and says "Hi!" A second later you and the child are running towards each other with arms outstretched in welcome. Scooping the child up in your arms, you hug each other tightly.

"Put me down! Where've you been? I missed you!" says the child. So, kneeling down, you take a minute and tell the child why you haven't been around for a while, but that you're coming to the garden a lot from now on. "Promise?" asks the child. "Yes," you say, and begin telling the child all of the things you want to do together. And as you look at the face of this little one, you realize where you've seen that face before. This child's face is your own face; there beside you stands your own precious, beautiful child self.

"I've found a lot of neat stuff! Do you want to see it?" asks the child. Of course, you say. And so all afternoon the child helps you learn how to skip again and look at bugs and climb trees and explore the woods and sit on the grass making up stories about the shapes of clouds and do, well, lots of things.

All too soon it seems, you realize that you need to get back to the world of grown-ups.

"When are you coming back to our garden?" asks your child. "Soon," you say, "very soon."

"Promise?" And you promise. The child gives you a big hug and kiss and runs off to explore and play some more.

Before you leave your garden, go back and sit in your chair for a minute and think about this garden and you and your child. What are you going to do together the next time you visit? . . . When are you coming back to your garden? . . . Choose something from your garden to take back with you to your grown-up world of worries and responsibilities and projects and to-do lists.

You begin to smile as you think about you and your child playing together in the garden again.

Now close your eyes as you sit in your chair in your garden. You can come back here as often as you wish. All you have to do is simply close your eyes and say the words, "I am in my garden now!" and you will be there.

Take three deep breaths in and out. Let go of any tension you are feeling about coming back to the world of grown-ups. As you exhale the third time, come back to this room, and when you are ready open your eyes.

2) After everyone is awake and alert, ask them to remain sitting quietly and to write down any feelings, thoughts, experiences, and impressions they have had during this journey to the garden.

3) If people wish, have them share their insights with each other in small groups.

VARIATIONS

• This activity can have a greater impact on participants if you perform it outdoors, where people can actually feel the grass between their toes and the wind and sun on their faces.

- If you feel participants are ready to try this kind of process on their own, have small groups of 4–5 people do a round-robin kind of guided meditation about the child's garden. You begin the meditation, get them to the garden, have them meet their child, and then let each person in the small group continue telling a part of what's happening in the garden. (This is similar to the **Story Circles** activity.)

NOTES

- In meditations of this sort I do not recommend that people lie down because they often fall asleep.

- When I lead workshops, it's always been a great joy for me to be around families with young children. On a crisp and blustery Sunday afternoon one March, a bunch of us (kids and adults) hiked around a hilly state park, discovering half-frozen waterfalls, throwing boomerangs, and sharing other wonders together. One little boy in our group, at that time about five years old, became a real expert in getting rides on the shoulders of all the grown-ups. After he had been riding on my shoulders for a while, he looked down at me from his lofty perch (I'm about 6' 4") and with great excitement shouted, "Boy! This is like being on top of a walking tree!"

  About three months later I finally realized how powerful and significant this one experience with this one child had been for me. I now had found a truly wonderful, very physical image of what it meant to be a childlike grown-up. I could now begin to see a beautiful picture of my own child self riding along perched atop my own very grown-up shoulders, with the child having the higher and often clearer view of what needs to be real and important in my grown-up life.

9 CHILDREN R 2

With the help of a special card deck, participants reflect on the qualities they most admire in children and then go around introducing themselves to each other *as* those childlike qualities.

GOALS

To reflect on the qualities people most admire in children.

To look at how these childlike qualities and attitudes can benefit grown-ups.

To think of ways to put more of these qualities into practice.

GROUP SIZE

Unlimited

TIME FRAME

10–15 minutes

MATERIALS NEEDED

One or more decks of the **Facilitator Childlike Quality Cards,** enough for one card per person; **Childlike Grown-up Affirmation Cards** (optional).

PROCESS

1) Before the workshop begins, make the card decks by enlarging and photocopying the five sheets that follow this activity onto colored cardstock (*bright* fluorescent colors work best). **Note:** When cut apart, the five sheets of colored cardstock will produce *one* deck of seventy different childlike quality cards. If you

expect more than seventy people at any of your workshops or presentations, prepare extra decks of cards as well. Be sure to use a different bright-colored cardstock for each deck so that you can easily sort the card decks before you next lead this activity. To enhance the appearance and durability of the cards, laminate the photocopied card sheets before cutting them apart into the seventy separate cards.

2) Ask participants what qualities and attitudes they most admire in children. Write their answers on the board or have them discuss the question in small groups. Make sure you point out the important difference between child*ish*—the somewhat selfish and negative behaviors most children grow out of—and child-*like*—the positive qualities and behaviors of children that need to be kept and cherished as people grow older.

3) Mention that the special cards you are holding reflect a number of these very important childlike qualities.

4) Ask each person to take a single card. (Use up all the cards in one color deck before you pass out the next deck.)

5) Say the following: "Reflect for a moment about what the quality on the card you are holding means to you. Then think of a time when you may have noticed this quality, activity, or attitude in a real child.

6) After a while, ask the following questions:

   ✔ What does this quality mean to you now as a grown-up?

   ✔ How could this quality or attitude benefit you each day?

7) Give the following instructions:

   ➤ Wander around the room and introduce yourselves to as many other people as you can, using only the name of your childlike quality. For instance, "Hi! I'm Fearless (or Exuberant or Giggly or Rambunctious, etc.)"

   ➤ If you wish, trade cards with each other for variety.

8) Collect all the cards at the end of this activity.

VARIATIONS

* Ask participants to share with each other how certain childlike qualities can really help grown-ups.

* Have participants share ideas with each other for encouraging more of a particular quality in daily life.

* Have people specifically reflect on how a certain childlike quality can benefit them at work each day.

* Have people line up in alphabetical order by the words on the cards and rapidly and loudly repeat the words after they are lined up. (If you have more than seventy people, form separate lines by the different colors of cards).

* Share and discuss the qualities in small groups of 4–6 people.

* Ask small groups of 4–5 people to string their qualities together as a jazzy kind of group or team name. For example, the "Creative-Amazed-Funny-Musical Group." Have the groups introduce themselves to the other groups with these names.

* Get people to think about what barriers get in the way of grown-up people experiencing and expressing a particular childlike quality.

* Enlarge and photocopy the **Childlike Grown-up Affirmation Cards** onto brightly-colored cardstock and hand out to participants to take home with them. Each sheet can then be cut apart and turned into a deck of seventy small cards that people can use to remind themselves of ways to be more childlike each day.

NOTES

* The master list from which I have selected these seventy qualities now numbers well over a hundred. Each group with whom I work usually comes up with a few new words and phrases that I almost always make a point of adding to my ongoing list.

- An elementary school teacher I know has chosen a few qualities that he always looks for in the children who enroll in his classroom each year, qualities such as zestfulness, compassion, and creativity. During each week, he goes out of his way to see these positive qualities in each one of the children and reflects back what he sees to the children and their parents.

Since we most often see what we believe we will see, this activity helps grown-ups affirm for themselves a whole range of valuable qualities they may want to experience in their lives.

RESOURCES

Growing Young. (2nd edition). Ashley Montagu. Among other insights, this book documents why the neotenous (childlike) qualities are so essential and beneficial to the human species.

You. A film from Cally Curtis Company. This delightful film about the qualities of children shows a baby exploring a roomful of "treasures." It makes most people think, and smile, and can be used as a wonderful icebreaker and discussion starter. Available for rental or purchase by calling 800/522-2559 (213/467-1101 in California). Ask for a copy of their latest catalog of other films and videos.

Absorbed	Bright
Adventurous	Bubbly
Affectionate	Capable
Amazed	Carefree
Believing	Cheerful
Blissful	Colorful
Bouncy	Compassionate

Creative	*Expressive*
Discovering	*Exuberant*
Eager	*Fanciful*
Energetic	*Fearless*
Enthusiastic	*Feeling*
Experimental	*Flexible*
Exploring	*Forthright*

Free	*Growing*
Fresh	*Happy*
Friendly	*Helpful*
Frolicsome	*Imaginative*
Funny	*Ingenious*
Giggly	*Innocent*
Gregarious	*Inquisitive*

Joyful	Now
Laughing	Open
Lively	Optimistic
Loving	Original
Lyrical	Perceptive
Musical	Persistent
Natural	Physical

Playful	Spontaneous
Rambunctious	Surprising
Refreshing	Tireless
Resilient	Touching
Sensitive	Trusting
Sharing	Wondering
Silly	Zestful

CHILDLIKE GROWN-UP AFFIRMATION CARDS

◆   Carefully cut out the seventy individual affirmation cards along the
    lines. (For durability laminate the sheet of cards before cutting.) Keep
    the cards in a small basket or container of some sort.

◆   Regularly choose one or more cards at random to see which qualities
    have "accidentally" come to your attention.

◆   As you go about your life as a grown-up that day, see how many
    opportunities you can discover or create to express the specific
    childlike quality or qualities you have chosen.

◆   These affirmation cards can also help people share ideas, thoughts,
    and feelings. Have each person in a family or group draw a card and
    talk about what that quality means to her or him.

ABSORBED	COMPASSIONATE
ADVENTUROUS	CREATIVE
AFFECTIONATE	DISCOVERING
AMAZED	EAGER
BELIEVING	ENERGETIC
BLISSFUL	ENTHUSIASTIC
BOUNCY	EXPERIMENTAL
BRIGHT	EXPLORING
BUBBLY	EXPRESSIVE
CAPABLE	EXUBERANT
CAREFREE	FANCIFUL
CHEERFUL	FEARLESS
COLORFUL	FEELING

FLEXIBLE	NATURAL
FORTHRIGHT	NOW
FREE	OPEN
FRESH	OPTIMISTIC
FRIENDLY	ORIGINAL
FROLICSOME	PERCEPTIVE
FUNNY	PERSISTENT
GIGGLY	PHYSICAL
GREGARIOUS	PLAYFUL
GROWING	RAMBUNCTIOUS
HAPPY	REFRESHING
HELPFUL	RESILIENT
IMAGINATIVE	SENSITIVE
INGENIOUS	SHARING
INNOCENT	SILLY
INQUISITIVE	SPONTANEOUS
JOYFUL	SURPRISING
LAUGHING	TIRELESS
LIVELY	TOUCHING
LOVING	TRUSTING
LYRICAL	WONDERING
MUSICAL	ZESTFUL

© 1993 Whole Person Associates 210 W Michigan Duluth MN 55802-1908 (218) 727-0500

10   FOOD GROUPS

Small groups are asked to list foods they think belong to the four "kid" food groups and, on some occasions, to actually sample some of these "kid" foods.

GOALS

To invent creative ways of using "kid foods" as a means of triggering positive childlike qualities and attitudes.

To enjoy (at least once in a while) foods that children really like.

GROUP SIZE

Unlimited, in small groups of 4–5 people

TIME FRAME

10 minutes

MATERIALS NEEDED

Crayons and/or watercolor markers; pencils; paper; flipchart and marker or blackboard and chalk (optional).

PROCESS

1) Use a twoing activity or some other method to help participants form small groups of 4–5 people.

2) Introduce this activity by first finding out how many people remember the four food groups they probably learned about in elementary school. You may want to write answers to this question on the board or flipchart.

3) Ask each group to come up with what they think children (and the child inside each person) consider the four food groups to be.

4) Have participants use crayons and markers to draw pictures of these four "kid food groups."

5) While people are drawing together also have them brainstorm and write down ways to include more of these kid foods (in appropriate amounts) in our daily lives, especially in healthy ways that help people stay in touch with their childlike, playful natures. (For an example, see the two stories and discussion under **Notes.**)

6) Have each group share their pictures and ideas on how to involve these foods in their lives each day.

VARIATIONS

- Have modest amounts of child foods available during breaks, along with healthier snack items. Tootsie Roll Pops® are usually very popular.

- During all-day workshops, suggest that people choose one item (however small or symbolic) from one of the kid food groups during the lunch period. Have the adult in them give the child in them permission to really savor that item.

- Before beginning this activity, secretly give one or two people a small bag of chocolate chip cookies, Hershey Kisses®, Tootsie Roll Pops®, or other items from one of the four kid food groups. Inform everyone that among them are one or two "Secret [fill in the name of the kid food item] People." Then say the following: "You can find out who these folks are by going up to other people and asking, 'Are you the Secret [kid food item] Person?' When the answer is 'Yes!' the Secret [kid food item] Person then gives you one of the kid food items." This variation works best, not as a separate activity, but as a playful thread woven throughout a whole workshop. It gives people just one more excuse to walk up to someone they don't know (yet) with smiles on their faces.

NOTES

- As grown-ups we sometimes have to consciously go out of the way to create reminders of our need to stop and smell the roses. Certain familiar and beloved foods from childhood can readily trigger pleasant associations and help people better access their childlike natures. The child in us still needs graham crackers and a glass of cold milk (as well as a nap) each afternoon.

- At one of my workshops a person told me she went out and bought the biggest bottle of industrial-strength pain reliever pills she could find, threw away all of the pills, refilled the bottle with jelly beans, and then put the bottle on her desk at work. When people with pounding headaches came by her desk and saw the bottle (assuming it contained painkillers), they would ask her if they could borrow a couple. She always said "Sure!" and then delighted in watching their reactions (usually laughter) when the jelly beans poured out into their hands. That bottle of jelly beans on her desk stimulated healthy laughter, regarded by more and more medical experts as an excellent natural painkiller and a "wonder drug with no harmful side effects."

- On occasion, people have reminded me that for many people overeating is an addiction as serious as alcoholism, and that tempting people with kid foods at a workshop is not supportive of new directions some individuals are trying to take. I respect and empathize with these realities. I certainly do not intend for this activity to contribute to anyone's distress. However, part of any recovery program involves people taking more responsibility for their choices and actions, and this principle applies when choosing whether or not to eat a cookie, gumdrop, or piece of chocolate at a play workshop.

RESOURCES

How to Eat Like a Child (And Other Lessons in Not Being a Grown-up). Delia Ephron.

Penn & Teller's How to Play with Your Food. Penn Jillette and Teller.

11   SWEET SOMETHINGS

Each participant has an opportunity to repeatedly hear a variety of positive messages that reinforce, nurture, and affirm the specialness and preciousness of his or her child spirit.

GOAL

To experience positive and affirming thoughts for nurturing the inner child.

GROUP SIZE

18–20 people per group

TIME FRAME

15–20 minutes

MATERIALS NEEDED

Chairs for half the group; gentle and soothing background music; cassette tape or CD player; tissues; paper and markers (optional).

PROCESS

1) Ask half the group to sit in a circle of chairs, facing inward. Have the other half of the group remain standing and spread out around the seated circle, placing their hands on the shoulders of the people sitting in front of them. (In the case of an odd number of people, make sure everyone seated is being touched by at least one hand of a standing person.)

2) Ask each person, standing and sitting, to think of at least two positive thoughts or affirmations they would like the child within

them to hear, perhaps words they wish they could have heard when they really were children.

3) To get the most out of the experience, ask the people seated to close their eyes. Sometimes the group seated may also want to hold hands with each other.

4) Begin softly playing the background music.

5) Have the standing people lean down and softly whisper one of their own affirmations into the ears of the seated people. Then each standing person moves to the right and whispers that same affirmation into the ear of the next seated person. This process continues until the standing people arrive back where they started.

6) If there is time, have the standing people go around again, but with a new affirmation.

7) Have participants silently switch roles and repeat the process once again.

☞ *Make sure the new standing people know that they should whisper an affirmation they would most like to hear, either one of their own or one they heard while sitting down.*

VARIATIONS

- Before beginning the activity, ask people to think of negative words and disempowering phrases that children sometimes hear, that maybe they heard when they were little. Tell them to write these negative words in big, bold letters on a sheet of paper, then to hold up their papers so that the others can read their words. Then have them wad up their papers and make a point of throwing them away into a (preferably large) garbage can (where they belong).

- Or, have each person write out the negative words and phrases on a piece of paper, wad the paper up *without* showing it to anyone else, and throw the wad at someone. These people then pick up the wad of paper, read it, decide whether or not they want to hold onto that negative thought, wad it up again, and throw it at someone else. After a minute or so of this sometimes heartfelt activity, throw the wads of paper into the garbage can, emphasizing that these words really *are* garbage and telling the group that now they are going to replace them with something positive.

- When the circle activity is over, it is helpful and even necessary to allow adequate time for people to share with each other what they experienced. An ideal way to do this is to first have people quietly write down their thoughts and feelings, noting the words they remembered and liked the most. Then have participants share with each other in small groups or with the whole group.

NOTES

- Part of learning to be more playful as grown-ups includes accepting, healing, and letting go of wounds and hurts from our childhoods. But it also involves replacing those negatives with something better. This activity is a powerful experience for many people. It often produces tears of sadness and joy as people experience hearing and saying positive affirmations instead of the negative ones they may have been bombarded with during their lives.

- Many people experience this process very deeply. During the activity I recommend that the people standing always maintain a continuity of physical contact with the people seated in front of them. In other words, when they get ready to shift their hands to the next person, have them make sure that they only move one hand at a time so that the people they just spoke to always feel someone's hand on their shoulders.

RESOURCES

My favorite music to use during this activity is *Fairy Ring* by Mike Rowland. A good source of this and other refreshing, relaxing, energizing, and positively-oriented music is *Heartbeats* catalog, available from Backroads Distributors by calling 800/825-4848.

© 1993 Whole Person Associates   210 W Michigan   Duluth MN 55802-1908 (218) 727-0500

12 THAT'S MY KID!

Participants focus on pictures of themselves as small children to affirm the beauty and playfulness of their inner child.

GOAL

To acknowledge the wonder and preciousness of the inner child.

GROUP SIZE

Small groups of 5–7 people

TIME FRAME

10–15 minutes

MATERIALS NEEDED

None provided by the facilitator.

PROCESS

1) Let participants know before the workshop begins to bring in a picture of themselves as a small child.

2) Have participants form small circles of 4–6 people and show their pictures to each other. People may also want to share something they remember from their childhoods when they were the age portrayed in their pictures.

3) Suggest to the whole group that when they go home they may want to frame the pictures they brought with them and place them on their desks at work or with all those other pictures of real children important to them. Then when colleagues and friends come up and ask who the new child is, people can smile proudly and (truthfully) say, "That's my kid!"

VARIATIONS

- Using loops of masking tape on the backs of the pictures, simply post the pictures on the wall at the beginning of the workshop. Later on ask participants to identify who's who in the child gallery.

- If the picture could talk, what would that child from years ago be saying to the grown-up person holding it? You might want people to write down these words (see also **Letter From Camp**).

- Have each person give a special name or nickname to the inner child he or she is rediscovering. The name might be an affectionate one from childhood or something brand new that expresses the essence of that child self.

NOTES

- This is a powerful activity, especially if people really do frame their pictures and put them where they can see them each day.

- Although this activity works best when people bring real pictures from childhood, not everyone can always find one. These people may want to find a picture of a child from a magazine that somehow reminds them of themselves as children.

RESOURCES

On Peter Alsop's album *Take Me with You!* the song titled "Take Me" provides a wonderful and funny sing-along opportunity for participants to affirm and reinforce the voice of that small child who wants to go with them everywhere they go. (See **Camp Songs** for address and phone number.)

13   WHEN YOU WERE LITTLE

Participants share with partners at least one positive memory of something they did to play and have fun when they were kids.

GOALS

To remember positive experiences from childhood, especially those involving play and fun, and how it felt during those activities.

To acknowledge the need to include activities in grown-up life that encourage the same positive feelings people had as children.

GROUP SIZE

Unlimited, in pairs

TIME FRAME

10–15 minutes

MATERIALS NEEDED

None

PROCESS

1) Have people find a partner using a twoing activity. If there is an "odd" person left over, you or someone helping out with the workshop can pair up with that person for this activity.

2) Acknowledge the fact that each person in the room has a very lively child self inside her or him who, like Peter Pan, never wants to (and really shouldn't) grow up.

3) Give the following instructions:

© 1993 Whole Person Associates   210 W Michigan   Duluth MN 55802-1908   (218) 727-0500

➤ Think of a time when you actually were a real child, picking any time from birth up to (but not including) puberty.

➤ Now think of something you did as a child that was a lot of fun for you, something that really was play. It may have been some way you played alone, with other kids on the block, or with friendly grown-ups in the neighborhood. Think about how you felt when you were playing.

4) Ask one person in the pair to go first, and the other person to just thoughtfully listen while the first person shares what he or she did and felt. Allow 1–2 minutes for this first sharing.

5) Tell participants to reverse roles when they hear the chime or whistle, but to wait for the signal so that the first person has enough time to share.

6) Ring the chime or blow the whistle and ask participants to switch roles. Allow another 1–2 minutes for this second sharing.

7) Ask the whole group how many people remembered something they did as children that they hadn't thought of for a long while. Usually quite a few hands will go up. Then ask those people if they would go out tomorrow or on the weekend and do that activity again. People usually laugh when they hear that.

VARIATIONS

• Have the group create a list of as many or all of the specific activities people remembered. This list could be especially helpful for people who have a hard time remembering how they had fun as children and want some suggestions to go out and try as grown-ups.

• Have the whole group generate a visible list of the kinds of feelings people had when they were playing or having fun as children. This list can serve as a useful springboard into a variety of other discussions about what grown-ups can do to become more childlike each day.

- Ask people to share with each other in pairs who one of their favorite grown-ups was when they were little, and especially *why* this person was so special to them. If there is time after the paired sharing, make a group list of the reasons why these grown-ups were so special so that people can really see all of the marvelous ways that grown-ups can affirm real children.

NOTES

- This activity offers participants a chance to reconnect with at least *one* time when they as children felt really playful, free, and alive. Use it to remind people that as grown-ups we all still need to find simple activities and experiences that can rekindle those same kinds of powerful and pleasurable feelings from childhood. Sometimes these activities are ones we remember doing as children, such as kite-flying. Other activities are the ones we invent and choose now, especially with the playful help of other childlike grown-ups!

- It's often helpful for us as facilitators to remind ourselves that for an often incredibly wide variety of reasons, many people at our workshops do not remember their childhoods with any degree of pleasure, and may in fact have to dig quite a bit to find even one memory that is pleasurable for them. However, this kind of activity is *not* intended to serve as therapy for anyone who still needs to heal from sometimes overwhelmingly painful child-hood experiences.

- The alternate activity about naming favorite grown-ups, sug-gested under **Variations,** can be a powerful experience. I've found that many of the reasons why particular grown-ups were special to people when they were children sound suspiciously like a list of childlike qualities. Various people in groups have told me that a grown-up was special for being ". . . a good listener, enthusiastic, creative, funny, a model of joy in living, kind, encouraging, loving, unusual, intuitive, magical, caring, accepting, sensitive, exuberant, nurturing, a storyteller, interesting, always positive," and so on. Naming favorite grown-ups and saying why they were so special can help people begin to positively evaluate their own "inner adults," seeing if that part of them treats their "inner child" with all of the nurturing, love, and respect that real children deserve and need.

RESOURCES

Homecoming: Reclaiming and Championing Your Inner Child. John Bradshaw.

Reclaiming the Inner Child. Edited by Jeremiah Abrams.

Recovery of Your Inner Child. Lucia Capacchione.

The Tao of Pooh. Benjamin Hoff.

In cooperative games I feel left in.

Terry Orlick

GETTING PHYSICAL

14 A HOP, A SKIP & A JUMP (p 56)

Participants spend a few minutes moving around the room in the uninhibited, gleeful manner of children. (4–5 minutes)

15 CAMP SONGS (p 58)

The whole group sings favorite childhood and other songs as a way of celebrating the power of song and discarding old beliefs about one's ability to sing. (5–15 minutes)

16 AH, CHUTE! (p 62)

In groups of 20–45 people, participants experience and improvise a variety of playful games using a large surplus parachute. (10–15 minutes)

17 GRUG (p 67)

Participants remind themselves of the many healthy ways in which humans can hug each other, and then in small groups invent unique group hugs. (5–10 minutes)

18 MILLER'S REEL (p 70)

Stimulated by vigorous, lively, and high energy music, groups of 25–30 people hold hands and improvise movements together. (5 minutes)

19 LEAF PILE (p 73)

Participants experience the delightful and delicious physical feeling of letting go and safely flying through the air. (10–15 minutes)

20 RHYTHM BAND (p 75)

Using a variety of inexpensive musical instruments, household implements, and other sources of sound, participants make joyful noises together. (5–10 minutes)

14   A HOP, A SKIP & A JUMP

Participants spend a few minutes moving around the room in the uninhibited, gleeful manner of children.

GOALS

To physically act like children.

To notice barriers that keep people from acting childlike.

GROUP SIZE

Unlimited

TIME FRAME

4–5 minutes

MATERIALS NEEDED

None

PROCESS

1) Ask people to spend a few minutes just skipping, hopping, or jumping around the room.

2) After a while, have participants gather in small groups to share what they experienced physically, mentally, and emotionally while performing this activity.

VARIATIONS

• You could bring out jump ropes for people to use. However, the presence of jump ropes often pushes the focus of the activity into a certain type of "skilled" competitiveness. Some people are excellent jumpers, others like to maintain control as turners, but most people just stand around watching the others play. Many people did not like this kind of playground activity when they were kids and may not enjoy it now.

- Have people pretend that they are children who have just learned to walk and totter around the room on their new legs.

NOTES

- Please try this exercise yourself before asking a group to do it. I discovered that I really enjoyed the physical activity of skipping, that wonderful feeling of floating down a trail. What I found hard was the fear of looking foolish and feeling embarrassed in front of other people. For exactly that reason, this simple-looking exercise may stimulate a lot of thoughts and feelings in many participants about what it really takes for grown-up people to be more childlike more often.

- I heard a story about a man who used to run and jog a lot, until he injured his leg. He couldn't run anymore, but he discovered that he could still skip. So he and some of his former running buddies decided to skip together as a way to exercise and have fun. What he also discovered was that when you skip, you almost always smile.

- After the exercise, tell people that they will now probably start noticing how natural a part of life skipping is for young children. It's as if there is some kind of skipping gene that gets activated when we're young. Who says we must turn off that joyous, creative, life-affirming impulse to hop, skip, and jump?

15   CAMP SONGS

The whole group sings favorite childhood and other songs as a way of celebrating the power of song and discarding old beliefs about one's ability to sing.

GOALS

To sing out loud and overcome nervousness in people who believe they can't sing.

To remember favorite childhood songs.

To have a lot of fun singing together as a group.

GROUP SIZE

Unlimited

TIME FRAME

5–15 minutes

MATERIALS NEEDED

Cassette tape player, cassette tapes and/or songbooks, piano and other musical instruments (optional).

PROCESS

1) Ask the people in the group who like to sing to raise their hands. At this point you may see only a few hands go up. Remind the group that your question wasn't how many people *can* sing, but how many people *like to sing*! Then ask the question again, and you will probably see many more hands go up.

2) Ask the group to suggest some of their favorite songs from childhood, especially ones people remember singing together at camp. Whenever possible, ask the person who suggested the song to lead the group in singing it.

☞ *The object of this activity is not to sing lots of verses of one song but to have fun and get people back into the child-at-camp spirit.*

VARIATIONS

* Have the group sing along, especially on rousing choruses, to tapes of such beloved children's singers as Peter, Paul, and Mary; Peter Alsop; John McCutcheon; and Raffi.
* Have people bring in musical instruments to help lead the singing. (Also see the **Rhythm Band** exercise.)
* Simple round singing can be a lot of fun with groups that want to stretch themselves a bit.

NOTES

* Not every group will have people in it who want to lead or help you lead songs. If you think *you* can't sing, you may want to practice with someone who has a piano or guitar to master some basic songs and feel more confident in leading others.
* Although you can make a big deal with this exercise by using a piano, guitar, songbooks for everyone, four-part harmony, etc., I recommend that you always keep it as simple as possible. Camp songs were meant to be easily remembered and sung without fancy instruments, and it is that spirit you are trying to recapture in this activity. Avoid doing anything that gets people once again feeling self-conscious and inadequate when it comes to their musical, lyrical abilities.

RESOURCES

John Holt's Book and Music Store. A wonderful source of books, tapes, and materials that parents, teachers, and other grown-ups can use to help make learning a joyful and lifelong exploration. For a free catalog, contact: Holt Associates, 2269 Massachusetts Avenue, Cambridge, MA 02140. 617/864-3100.

Kids Songs and *Kid Songs 2 ("*Holler-Along Handbooks" complete with cassette tapes) by Nancy and John Cassidy. Each of these delightful and durable songbooks "for anyone age four to forever" has a tape cassette attached, and will help you and your groups recapture the magic of children's songs. The first book contains one of my all-time favorite songs, *Puff (The Magic Dragon)*. Available in bookstores or by ordering through *The Flying Apparatus Catalog* from Klutz Press, 2121 Staunton Court, Palo Alto, CA 94306. 415/424-0739.

Kylie's Song and *Kylie's Concert*. Patty Sheehan. Illustrations by Itoko Maeno. Who says koala bears can't sing? Or help save the world?

Music for Little People Catalog. Books, tapes, stories, puppets, videos, musical instruments, and other family-tested materials for children of all ages. Call 800/727-2233 for a free catalog.

Wha'D'Ya Wanna Do? Take Me With You! Stayin' Over. Peter Alsop. Each of these three cassette albums (14 songs each) goes straight to the heart of children's concerns and curiosities, and stimulates imagination, creativity, and much laughter. The songs are also great for grown-ups, both as a way to connect with real children and as a wonderfully stimulating exploration of the playful child self each of us was and is. A detailed activity guide packaged with each tape contains all words and music chords, as well as suggested discussion questions and activities for use with the songs. To order a catalog of cassette tapes, videos, songbooks and other materials, contact: Peter Alsop, P.O. Box 960, Topanga, CA 90290. 213/455-2318.

16 AH, CHUTE!

In groups of 20–45 people, participants experience and improvise a variety of playful games using a large surplus parachute.

GOAL

To have fun playing with a large parachute, including making up new ways to play with it.

GROUP SIZE

Up to 40–45 people (per parachute)

TIME FRAME

10–15 minutes

MATERIALS NEEDED

One 28-foot-diameter surplus parachute (one chute for every 40–45 people).

PROCESS

1) Walk out into the center of the group carrying the parachute (still enclosed in its tote box, stuff sack, or duffel bag). Tell the group that inside the container is one of the most effective props for stimulating group play ever invented. Then, with a grand flourish, drop or toss the container, step back, and let the group unpack and unfurl the parachute.

2) Before suggesting any of your own activities, let the group start playing spontaneously with the chute and just see what happens. Encourage their ideas about what games to play with the chute.

3) After a few minutes, you will probably want to lead the group in some of your favorite activities. (See **Variations** for a few of my favorite ways to play with the chute.)

4) As a closing activity, have everyone hold onto the chute with both hands, slowly lean back together, and find that balance point where everyone is supporting everyone else. (Whenever possible have people grip the edges of the chute where the nylon cords are sewn all the way to the center.) While everyone is still leaning back and holding onto the parachute, you might also ask them to slowly move their bodies to the right or left and create a wavelike effect around the chute.

5) Ask the group to shake out and pack up the parachute together. Not only does this help you save some time, but letting the group decide how to roll and stuff the chute back into its original container becomes another playful activity in itself.

VARIATIONS

- **Popcorn.** Lay the chute flat on the ground and place small soft objects (such as rolled-up socks or Nerf® balls) on top of the chute. Tell people that this is a popcorn popper and these objects are the kernels of corn. Have them apply the "heat" by moving the chute up and down. It usually doesn't take long before the kernels are popping high into the air.

- **Surfing.** Have people quickly raise and lower the chute in a continuous wave around the circle. After this gets going, toss a medium-sized ball (something with a little weight to it) onto the surface of the chute and have people pass the ball around on the chute with the same kind of wave movement. You can also have participants try to keep the ball away from the center opening or make it a goal for them to reach.

- **Mountain Climbers.** Have people lift the chute up as high as they can in front of them, take two steps forward, and then kneel down on top of the edge of the chute. Let the "mountain" of the chute billow up in front of them for a few moments and then have everyone pat it down together. (The air will slowly escape through the hole in the center.)

- **Animal Crossing.** Holding the parachute at waist level, count off to the right or left by threes or fours, not by numbers, but by *animals*. On your signal, the group lowers the chute to the ground and then billows it up as high as possible. When the chute is at its peak, yell out the name of one of the animals. When those people hear their animal name they let go of the chute, run underneath, and find a place on the other side. After each animal person has had a chance to run underneath, call out two or even three animal names at a time. Suggest people make the noises of their animals as they run underneath.

  ☞ *Ask the group for names of animals native to where the workshop is being held. For example, participants in the American Southwest often suggest animals such as hawks, coyotes, rattlesnakes, lizards, jackrabbits, and roadrunners. The possibilities are endless.*

- **Tent.** Have people billow up the parachute, take three steps forward, pull the chute over their heads and *behind* their backs, and then sit down on the inside edge of the chute. By doing this a tent is created with everyone inside! This experience is usually amazing to most people, so let everyone savor being inside the tent together before going back outside. Some people may want to stand up in the center hole and look out at the wonderful shape the group has created.

- **Sleeping Bag.** Everyone lies on the floor like spokes on a wheel, with feet pointing to the center. People pull the parachute up to their chins and look at all the other heads peeking out of the giant sleeping bag.

- **Shark.** Have people sit down around the edge of the chute, facing the center, and pull the chute up over their legs to their waists. (Always give the group the option of sitting down on the floor, on chairs, or a combination of both.) Tell them that the surface of the parachute they are holding onto is really the ocean, and that each person there is a sunbather innocently dangling his or her legs off the side of a raft on a beautiful sunny day.

Ask for one volunteer to be the shark. The role of the shark in this exercise (of course!) is to cruise around *underneath* the water (parachute), grab the legs or ankles of an unsuspecting bather, and pull that person screaming and struggling under the water. Remind the bathers that this game is *most* fun if they die as horrible, noisy, gruesome, and bloody a death as possible when they're being pulled under the water. During this process make sure all the bathers still seated on the edge billow the chute up and down vigorously (making high waves) so that no one knows exactly where the shark is.

After the shark has pulled a bather under the water, that person then also becomes a shark. These new sharks create other sharks until all the bathers have been pulled under the water. (When everyone has become a shark—before the group leaves the water and becomes human again—you might reflect for a moment on all of the misleading information, unfair treatment, and generally bad press sharks have received over the years!)

🖙 *This game could also be called "Swamp Thing" or "Alligator," with the innocent bathers dangling their legs in a river, lake, or bayou.*

- See the list of books under **Resources** for a number of other parachute activities, as well as other group games and activities.

NOTES

- I am often amazed at the new activities people invent while playing with the parachute. Be sure to make notes of these so that your own personal "Ah, Chute!" repertoire keeps expanding.

- Be sensitive to people who experience feelings of claustrophobia while underneath the chute during an activity.

- The 28-foot-diameter chute is an ideal size for most groups. Significantly larger diameter chutes tend to be too heavy and less versatile for use with smaller sized groups. You may also want to find a slightly smaller diameter chute if you work with groups smaller than 15–20 people.

- Parachutes can be purchased at very reasonable prices from most military surplus stores. To make the chute as safe as possible, cut off all metal fittings as well as the nylon cords that crisscross the center opening. Leave intact all the nylon cords that are sewn into the fabric of the chute, but clip off remnants of the nylon harness cords that may still be attached to the edge of the parachute.

- Surplus parachutes are really hard to hurt. From time to time, however, you may need to mend a tear in the ripstop nylon. To avoid mildew, rotting, and musty smells, make sure the chute is completely dry after you've washed it or used it outdoors.

RESOURCES

More New Games. Andrew Fluegelman, editor.

Playfair: Everybody's Guide to Noncompetitive Play. Matt Weinstein and Joel Goodman.

Raven Industries sells brightly-colored parachutes specially designed for heavy-duty use, ranging in size from 12 feet to 32 feet in diameter. For a free catalog call 800/227-2836.

Silver Bullets. Karl Rohnke. Available from Project Adventure, P.O. Box 100, Hamilton, MA 01936. 508/468-7981.

The New Games Book. Andrew Fluegelman, editor.

The Second Cooperative Sports & Game Book. Terry Orlick.

17 GRUG

Participants remind themselves of the many healthy ways in which humans can hug each other, and then in small groups invent unique group hugs.

GOAL

To allow small groups of people to playfully exchange healthy touch with each other.

GROUP SIZE

10–15 people

TIME FRAME

5–10 minutes

MATERIALS NEEDED

None

PROCESS

1) Have participants form groups of 10-15 people to demonstrate with each other different kinds of hugs they have observed people exchanging at some time or other.

 ☞ *You can find a variety of hugging methods, such as the A-Frame Hug, Ankle Hug, Bear Hug, Cheek-to-Cheek Hug, Sandwich Hug, Side-to-Side Hug, and so on, in Kathleen Keating's two hug books listed in the resources section of this exercise.*

2) After several minutes, ask each group to create together a very special and unique group hug (GRUG). This usually takes a few

minutes. If you have time, let each group then demonstrate their group hug to the other groups.

VARIATIONS

- Have groups talk with each other about the difference between healthy and unhealthy touch. (As Bob Czimbal and Maggie Zadikov point out in their book *Vitamin T*, when you take the "T" away from "TOUCH" you end up with "OUCH," or unhealthy touch.) Ask people what they liked or disliked about the different kinds of hugs they shared together. Have them discuss how people can share more healthy touch in different environments, such as family gatherings, school, work, meetings, and so on.

NOTES

- People need to understand that it is all right not to touch or be touched. Some participants at workshops are hungry for healthy touch, but for a variety of reasons feel hesitant or afraid to ask for or receive it. As facilitators sometimes all we can do is keep setting up safe opportunities for people to explore and experience, and then step back and let them be responsible for getting their needs met in ways that feel right for them.

RESOURCES

The Hug Therapy Book. Hug Therapy 2. Kathleen Keating. These two delightful books whimsically illustrate the joys and benefits of hugging, and include a dictionary of different types of hugs and a Certificate of Membership in the Institute of Hug Therapy.

Vitamin T: A Guide To Healthy Touch. Bob Czimbal and Maggie Zadikov. "Vitamin T is the nurturing nutrient found in healthy TOUCH. Natural sources of Vitamin T are handshakes, hugs, kisses, cuddles, and rubs obtained from family, friends, and co-workers. Megadoses are provided by massage. Positively habit-forming. Give with permission only. Guaranteed safe for all ages. Keep within reach of children." Available from: Open Book Publishers, 2501 SE Madison, Portland, OR 97214.

18 MILLER'S REEL

Stimulated by vigorous, lively, and high-energy music, groups of 25–30 people hold hands and improvise movements together.

GOAL

To energetically and spontaneously dance together as a group.

GROUP SIZE

20–25 people per group (playground)

TIME FRAME

5 minutes

MATERIALS NEEDED

Extremely lively, high-energy music—such as the activity's title song "Miller's Reel"; tape cassette or CD player.

PROCESS

1) Have participants form groups of 20–25 people.

2) Ask people to hold hands with the others in their group and simply move along together with the very lively music that you will play.

3) Start the music and let it play for 5 or more minutes.

VARIATIONS

- Play three or four selections of music and let the groups experiment with the different patterns of movement that each piece stimulates.

NOTES

- Since most musical selections only last about 2–3 minutes, you may want to repeat the first piece of music or have another one ready to play immediately after the first one ends. This gives each group a chance to really enjoy dancing and playing together, without wearing out too many people.

- Many people feel uncomfortable at not knowing how to dance. Avoid music which puts any pressure at all on people to perform dance steps in some prescribed way, such as square-dance music. This activity should provide an opportunity for people to simply move and improvise dance steps together.

- This activity works well even with large groups, as long as you form "playgrounds" of 20–25 people. I once conducted this activity on a large outdoor playing field with a conference group of about six hundred people. It was thrilling to see thirty playgrounds of people spontaneously dancing together and weaving in and out of other groups.

- You can easily find out which cassettes or CDs feature "Miller's Reel" (and are currently in print) by looking up that title in the most recent edition of your local record store's Phonolog catalog. Tapes or CDs which have "Miller's Reel" will also undoubtedly include other pieces of lively dance music. Any other high-energy music, however, should work well for this exercise.

RESOURCES

One fantastic album featuring "Miller's Reel" and many other pieces of extremely energetic country dance music is *Country Fiddle Band: One Hundred Years of Country Dance Music*, conducted by Gunther Schuller and originally published by Columbia Records in 1976 (Album # M33981). Unfortunately, this album is out of print, but it's so good that I recommend searching for the original LP or cassette tape in used record stores.

Also check out a piece titled "Dancing Under the Moon" (a wonderful 4 minute "merengue" dance number) by guitarist Ottmar Liebert on his album *Borrasca*.

19 LEAF PILE

Participants experience the delightful and delicious physical feeling of letting go and safely flying through the air.

GOAL

To have that childlike experience of flying through the air without worrying about getting hurt when you land.

GROUP SIZE

20–30 people

TIME FRAME

10–15 minutes

MATERIALS NEEDED

A minimum of 20–30 foam cushions (no springs).

PROCESS

1) Since most workshop rooms won't have enough (or any) cushions, this exercise generally works only if participants bring a cushion with them to the workshop. So arrange for this beforehand.

2) Pile up the cushions in a large heap, about three feet high and six feet across.

3) Have participants take turns running and leaping one at a time onto the pile of cushions. (You may want to station several people around the pile to help ensure the safety of the others leaping onto the cushions.)

4) See that everyone gets at least one turn to jump, and if you have enough time let participants make several jumps.

VARIATIONS

* A *maximum* of two participants may want to leap together.

NOTES

* With this much fun comes some potential for danger. This exercise works when people don't have to worry about hitting the floor. Please make sure that you have enough cushions and enough people who aren't jumping to help participants jump safely into the leaf pile.

20 RHYTHM BAND

Using a variety of inexpensive musical instruments, household implements, and other sources of sound, participants make joyful noises together.

GOAL

To have fun making music together.

GROUP SIZE

Groups of 20–25 people

TIME FRAME

5–10 minutes

MATERIALS NEEDED

Simple rhythm instruments and noise-makers.

PROCESS

1) If possible, ask people ahead of time to bring simple musical instruments or noise-makers along with them to the workshop. Otherwise, have your own bag of instruments available with such cheap items as kazoos, combs and wax paper, whistles, rattles, harmonicas, rhythm sticks, drums, and so on.

2) Have everyone select an instrument and experiment with the sounds it makes. Tell people they can trade with each other if they wish.

3) After a minute or so of this individual "tuning," ask the "band members" to gather into some kind of less-than-rigid formation and begin marching around making joyful noise together.

- Ask for volunteers to be band leaders. Have one person lead the band for 30–60 seconds, then ask another volunteer to lead.

VARIATIONS

- Have people sit down instead of moving around.
- Eliminate the instruments altogether and ask people to experiment with the various sounds and rhythms they can produce with their bodies (hands, feet, arms, mouth, etc.).

NOTES

- A wonderful kind of silliness occurs from this activity as grown-up people allow themselves to make noises just for the fun of it.

... the old man laughed loud and joyously, shook up the details of his anatomy from head to foot, and ended by saying that such a laugh was money in a man's pocket, because it cut down the doctor's bill like everything.

Mark Twain

LAUGHING FOR THE HEALTH OF IT

21 WHEN YOU'RE UP (p 80)

Participants physically experience the sometimes ludicrous conflict between mind and body that can occur when learning something new. (3–5 minutes)

22 HOOPLA (p 83)

Participants use Hula Hoops® or other large plastic rings as a way of playfully, physically, and energetically solving a problem together. (5–10 minutes)

23 INSTANT RECESS (p 87)

Using a positive variation of a familiar childhood game, participants get a chance to experience again the laughter, energy, and overall exuberance that is so characteristic of children. (3–4 minutes)

24 MAY WE HAVE THIS DANCE? (p 90)

Participants learn a new way of dancing "cheek to cheek" that helps loosen self-consciousness and inhibitions on the dance floor. (5 minutes)

25 MUSICAL LAPS (p 94)

In small groups, participants take the highly competitive game of Musical Chairs and add a twist that turns it into a highly energetic and cooperative activity. (5–7 minutes)

26 SOCK IT TO ME (p 97)

Using ordinary (but clean) socks, circles of 10–15 people get a chance to experience how good uproarious and sustained laughter feels. (5–10 minutes)

27 SPOONING (p 102)

Participants learn how to hang spoons on their noses as a way of confronting and pushing through barriers to becoming more playful. (5–10 minutes)

21 WHEN YOU'RE UP

Participants physically experience the sometimes ludicrous conflict between mind and body that can occur when learning something new.

GOALS

To generate laughter within the group.

To highlight the challenges of dealing with new information.

GROUP SIZE

Unlimited

TIME FRAME

3–5 minutes

MATERIALS NEEDED

Flipchart and markers or blackboard and chalk (optional); overhead
projector (optional); **When You're Up** overhead transparency
(optional).

PROCESS

1) Draw the **When You're Up** pattern of arrows, which follows this
   activity, on the blackboard or flipchart or use it as an overhead
   transparency.

2) Point to each of the arrows in the first row. As you point to each
   arrow ask people to say the direction the arrow is pointing.

3) Point to each of the arrows in the second row. As you point to
   each arrow ask people to move in the direction the arrow is
   pointing.

4) Point to each of the arrows in the third row. As you point to each arrow ask people to say the direction the arrow is pointing and simultaneously move in the opposite direction the arrow is pointing.

5) Point to each of the arrows in the fourth row. As you point to each arrow ask people to say the opposite direction the arrow is pointing, and simultaneously move in the direction the arrow is pointing.

6) Point to each of the arrows in the fifth row. As you point to each arrow ask people to say the direction and move in the direction the arrow is pointing.

NOTES

- The teacher who introduced me to this exercise said it provided a nice way for adults to experience how overwhelmed children can feel on the first day of school. It also playfully models the process most of us still go through even as grown-ups when we are attempting to master a new skill or behavior. This activity also usually generates a lot of laughter and is excellent as a physical icebreaker with most groups.

© 1993 Whole Person Associates   210 W Michigan   Duluth MN 55802-1908 (218) 727-0500

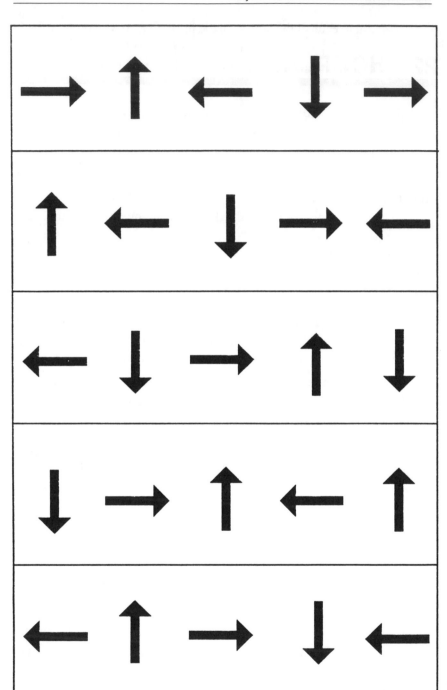

22 HOOPLA

Participants use Hula Hoops® or other large plastic rings as a way of playfully, physically, and energetically solving a problem together.

GOALS

To stimulate vigorous laughter and gentle physical movement.

To cooperatively solve a problem together.

GROUP SIZE

15–25 people per group

TIME FRAME

5–10 minutes

MATERIALS NEEDED

Two different colored hula hoops for each group (at least 25–28 inches in diameter); one tube sock per person (optional).

PROCESS

1) Ask participants to form a circle, facing inward. Depending on the size of the entire group, you may need to use a "twoing" exercise to get the group to split into two or more smaller groups of 15–25 people.

2) Holding the two hoops, walk into the center of the circle. You will almost always hear nervous or excited laughter rippling through the group as people see the hoops in your hands and begin thinking that some people are about to be asked to twirl those hoops around their waists—something most of us know

we can't do. You might mention this thought to the group and then reassure everyone that Hula Hoops® can be used in other interesting ways.

3) Have everyone join hands around the circle.

4) Ask two people in the circle to temporarily unclasp their hands. Hold the two hoops between them and then ask them to rejoin their hands through the hoops (so that the hoops are now resting on top of their joined hands.)

5) Tell the participants that you challenge them to simultaneously pass the two hoops in *opposite* directions around the circle without ever once unclasping their hands. One color hoop goes in one direction and the other color hoop goes in the opposite direction. The hoops cross in the middle and keep going, so that each color hoop ends up where the other hoop began.

6) Make sure everyone understands these basic instructions— especially the one about keeping their hands joined at all times— and then give a signal to begin.

7) As the exercise begins, you may overhear some comments about the challenge being impossible, especially the part about the hoops crossing in the middle. Don't say anything at this point; let the people in the group encourage themselves and solve the problem together.

8) When the two hoops have gone all the way around the circle, ask the group a very important question, "Who won?"

VARIATIONS

- After the hoops have gotten back to where they started, encourage the group to share what they felt and experienced as they solved this playful challenge together. Ask them, "What helped solve the problem? What got in the way?" People often notice that what helps them solve the problem are the encouraging words from others, the cooperation, watching how other people

got the hoops around themselves, the laughter, and the willing-
ness to take some risks together. These kinds of insights can turn
this exercise into a useful team-building activity.

- Ask everyone in the circle, or every other person, to remain silent
  during the activity. This approach can be particularly useful if
  you have noticed ahead of time that a few people always seem to
  dominate the group and tell others what to do, often stifling
  group initiative and creative problem solving. (Just request
  silence. Avoid singling out any one person.)

- Have participants do the exercise with their eyes closed. I
  suggest you try this only after the group has first done it in the
  regular way.

- Instead of having everyone face the center of the circle, have
  people face outward. Or, have one person face outward, the next
  person face inward, and so on.

- I have found that with a few groups the suggestion to hold hands
  itself becomes a disruptive issue, most often with young males
  in junior high/middle school and high school. One way of
  eliminating this conflict is to have everyone in the circle hold
  onto the end of a tube sock, so that they are not touching hands
  with each other. This procedure also helps make the process of
  passing the hoops around the circle even more interesting.

NOTES

- This activity is a gentle but exciting icebreaker for most groups.
  The physical nature of the challenge quickly gets people in-
  volved, touching, and laughing heartily together.

- This activity can sometimes illuminate what people tend to say
  to themselves and others when faced with a challenge; how
  much they think they are allowed to help each other during the
  exercise; and whether or not they think it's okay to laugh as they
  try to solve a problem.

© 1993 Whole Person Associates   210 W Michigan   Duluth MN 55802-1908   (218) 727-0500

- The suggested diameter of the hoops is usually more than adequate for most people—even in skirts or kilts—to wiggle through without getting stuck.

- In most groups at least one or two people will not follow the instructions to keep their hands joined, often out of frustration or embarrassment at not being able to figure out how to do the activity. Usually the best thing to do is let it happen, although you may need to intervene to get the hoops moving again.

- With large groups you will have two or more smaller groups passing hoops at the same time. Many times these groups will automatically start competing with each other. This is usually playful enough, but you might want to point out afterwards that when you introduced this exercise you didn't say anything at all about one group having to win over another. Somehow the groups seemed to assume that competition was the rule. This could help stimulate an interesting discussion about the healthy and unhealthy nature of competition.

RESOURCES

Hula Hoops® may be purchased at most toy stores. If you travel as a facilitator/presenter and need as much portability as possible in your props, you can now buy collapsible plastic hoops. Six individual segments join together to make up one 28-inch-diameter plastic hoop, which costs little more than a regular hoop. For a free catalog containing this and other nifty toys and props, contact: Project Adventure, P.O. Box 100, Hamilton, MA 01936. 508/468-7981.

23 INSTANT RECESS

Using a positive variation of a familiar childhood game, participants get a chance to experience again the laughter, energy, and overall exuberance that is so characteristic of children.

GOAL

To stimulate a phenomenon known on many elementary school playgrounds as "group glee," a sudden and largely uncontrollable eruption of positive, unrestrained giggling, laughing, and running around.

GROUP SIZE

Unlimited

TIME FRAME

3–4 minutes

MATERIALS NEEDED

One tagging object for every 10–15 people. Use relatively soft items like Koosh® balls, Nerf® balls, bright-colored handkerchiefs, beach balls, balloons, etc.

PROCESS

1) Begin by asking the following questions:

   ✔ How many of you have ever played the game of Tag?

   ✔ How many of you enjoy sharing a friendly hug with another person?

2) Let the group know that they're about to play a game that combines the best parts of both hugging and Tag.

3) Ask for volunteers (about one for every 10–15 people).

4) Give each volunteer a tagging object.

5) Introduce this person (or persons) to the group as the "Playground Monitor," a role similar to "It" in the old game of Tag.

6) Explain the following rules:

➤ You are safe from being tagged by a Playground Monitor *only* if you are hugging *one* other person.

➤ You can only hug that one other person for five and a half seconds, then you need to go find a completely different person to hug.

➤ You are fair game for being tagged by a Playground Monitor when you are standing by yourself.

➤ Playground Monitors, you have to physically hold onto your tagging object and actually touch a person with it. For safety reasons, it's no fair (and no fun) to throw a tagging object at anyone.

➤ If you are tagged, you then become a Playground Monitor and take possession of a tagging object. The now ex-Playground Monitor is then free to go hug other people.

VARIATIONS

• After the shrieking and laughing have built to a crescendo, you might want to momentarily stop the group one or more times and say, "Now, you're only safe if you're hugging five (or ten or more) other people." Depending on the size of the group, you can end the exercise with everyone hugging everyone else in a giant group hug.

• A short while into the game, few people really care who has a tagging object. You may even want to collect all the tagging objects and just have everyone run around and hug each other.

NOTES

- I decided to call this exercise **Instant Recess** for one very good reason. If you walked up, closed your eyes, and listened to the shouts, screams, laughter, and movement going on, you would think you had stumbled into a group of fourth and fifth graders on a playground somewhere. Grown-up people rarely have a chance to experience this kind of full-hearted glee, which the dictionary defines as "jubilant gaiety and joy."

- People who have issues with touch or of being around loud sounds and unpredictable movements may feel uncomfortable, or even scared during this game. You may want to talk about these concerns with participants before the exercise begins. Ask the group for ways to help make the activity safe and fun for as many people as possible. Make sure participants know it's okay to hug in ways that are appropriate and comfortable for them.

© 1993 Whole Person Associates   210 W Michigan   Duluth MN 55802-1908 (218) 727-0500

24 MAY WE HAVE THIS DANCE?

Participants learn a new way of dancing "cheek to cheek" that helps loosen self-consciousness and inhibitions on the dance floor.

GOALS

To laugh and have a lot of fun while meeting and dancing with many other people.

To set aside feelings of shyness and awkwardness on the dance floor, including worries about "not knowing the right steps."

GROUP SIZE

Unlimited

TIME FRAME

5 minutes

MATERIALS NEEDED

Tape cassette or CD player; classic high-energy rock and roll music.

PROCESS

1) Begin by asking people what they really like about dancing. Comments often include such features as creative movement, being with other people, the music, aerobic workout, and spontaneity.

2) Then ask the group what they don't like about dancing. These comments range from not knowing the steps and feeling awkward to disliking noisy, loud, and smoky rooms, partners you don't want to dance with, and so on.

3) Tell the group that they are now going to have an opportunity to learn a new way of dancing that will hopefully "accentuate the positives" and at least partially eliminate the negatives.

4) Using a twoing activity, ask each person to go find a partner. (You may need to reassure men in the group that it's perfectly all right in the kind of dancing the group is about to do for guys to be partners with guys!) Have each "couple" find a place on the "dance floor" where they have a little space around them and can see you give a quick lesson in this new way to dance.

5) Give the following instructions:

➤ We will now get into the "basic dance position." Stand back to back with your partner and link your arms together. This, of course, eliminates any problem some of you may have in not wanting to look at your dance partner the whole time you are dancing.

➤ Next come the fancy dance steps. There aren't any! All you have to do is move your feet around.

6) Have each dance couple practice moving their feet in place for a few seconds (without music).

7) Have each couple practice dancing around the floor, arms linked back to back, rhythmically moving with (not against) their partner.

8) Say the following: "What if some other dancer catches someone's eye? Yes, that is also an important consideration. On this dance floor couples are encouraged to switch dance partners. But gracefully switching partners with another couple while dancing back to back *can* be a bit tricky. How can this be done smoothly and easily?"

9) To demonstrate how to switch partners, ask for two volunteer dance couples (Dance Couple #1 and Dance Couple #2). Have each demonstration couple assume the basic back-to-back dance position, and begin dancing around a little bit (without music).

10) As the couples are moving about, say the following: "Suddenly, across the crowded room, Dance Couple #1 catches the eyes of Dance Couple #2 and glides over to dance with them."

11) After the couples have actually danced over to each other and are dancing side by side, have Couple #1 say the following, "May we have this dance?"

12) Give the following instructions:

> ➤ The person from the other couple you are now standing *beside* is your new dance partner. Here's how to get to dance with that new partner.

> ➤ Each partner in each couple first unhooks his or her inside (in relation to the other couple) arm from their current partner and immediately rehooks that arm with the inside arm of their new dance partner.

> ➤ Then each partner unhooks their outside arm from their old partner and joins back-to-back with the new partner. Voila! A new dance partner selected with grace and style. The new couple then dances off together in search of new dance partners.

13) Ask if there are any questions. If necessary, have the two demonstration couples go through the moves once more. Then, before the *real* dance begins, ask the group to applaud Dance Couple #1 and Dance Couple #2 for their grace and style in leading the dance lesson.

14) Start the music! Try to get all the dancers to find as many new dance partners as they can before the music ends.

VARIATIONS

• Some groups may want you to play more than one song.

• Have couples link with other couples to form small dance groups of 4–6 people.

NOTES

* It's important that people be able to hear the music while they are dancing during this exercise. When I have to deal with inadequate public address systems, I have been known to take my portable boom box, balance it on my head, and walk around on the dance floor so more people can hear the music.

* With larger groups you may want 4–6 demonstration dance couples.

* After people have *first* assumed the basic back-to-back dance position with their partners, I usually like to mention that on *this* dance floor the group is about to give new meaning to the phrase "dancing cheek to cheek."

* Some people for their own various reasons will sit out the dance, and that is always OK with me.

* You could eliminate the demonstration of how to gracefully switch partners, but I really think it adds a lot of fun and excitement to the whole process and helps eliminate any fears people may have about not being able to do even this kind of dancing "right." Just make the demonstration as fun and fast as possible so that people can start dancing without a lot of delay.

* The main purpose of this dance is to have a lot of fun together. Be ready to step in and gently intervene if you see some people dragging their partners too fast or hard around the dance floor. This often happens when short and tall people end up as temporary dance partners.

RESOURCES

"True Love" and "La Bamba" are particularly excellent songs to use with this exercise. I also like "New Attitude" by Patti LaBelle.

© 1993 Whole Person Associates   210 W Michigan   Duluth MN 55802-1908 (218) 727-0500

25 MUSICAL LAPS

In small groups, participants take the highly competitive game of Musical Chairs and add a twist that turns it into a highly energetic and cooperative activity.

GOALS

To play together, instead of against each other.

To giggle, scream, laugh, and generally have a lot of fun marching around to lively music.

To enjoy healthy physical contact with other people in a group.

To demonstrate that it is possible to take a traditional game and turn it into a cooperative one filled with the kind of fun, thrills, and excitement people often seek in more competitive activities.

GROUP SIZE

Unlimited, with 10–12 people per small group

TIME FRAME

5–7 minutes

MATERIALS NEEDED

Tape cassette or CD player; high-energy music. "Stars and Stripes Forever" and other march music by John Phillip Sousa are always excellent choices.

PROCESS

1) Have participants form groups of 10–12 people. Ask each group to set up their little area for a game of Musical Chairs. (You'll

probably hear both cheers and groans when you announce this.) Of course, there's no "right" way to arrange the chairs, although the classic Musical Chairs arrangement traditionally starts off with one less chair than there are people playing. Some groups will form circles of chairs, others will line up the chairs facing in alternate directions, and so on.

2) Ask participants if they've ever played Musical Chairs. Have people share what they most loved about the game. Then have them say what they absolutely hated about the game.

3) Let people know that you have a special way of making that old game more exciting by changing just one of the rules.

4) First review together the "traditional" Musical Chair rules, so that everyone understands what is about to happen:

➤ Rule 1. When the music is playing, people stand up and move in one direction around the outside of the chairs.

➤ Rule 2. When the music stops, everyone tries to find a place to sit down. Since there is always one less chair less than the total amount of people, the person who couldn't find a seat is out of the game.

➤ Rule 3. After each round another chair is removed. The game continues until there are only two players left trying to sit in the final chair. The person who sits in the chair when the music stops wins the game.

5) Now make the following rule change. "In our game, however, no one gets kicked out. (Pause). Everyone still needs to find some place to sit down, though . . . (pause) . . . with fewer and fewer chairs.

6) Let the groups think for a moment about what you've just said. People usually realize very quickly that with fewer and fewer chairs they will soon be sitting on each other's laps! This insight often produces a lot of laughter in each group.

7) Start the music and let people begin marching. You're in charge of the pause button. As the game progresses and people pile up on fewer and fewer chairs, try to make sure everyone in each group is *really* sitting down somewhere before you play the music again.

VARIATIONS

- Have participants make up a set of new rules together to transform some other highly competitive game into something more cooperative.

NOTES

- It's generally a good idea to have no more than a dozen people playing together in each group. This helps participants keep from getting crushed by too many people, and also helps avoid breaking or damaging chairs in whatever facility you are using.

- Even with the rule change, some people in many groups still race around competitively, and even dangerously, trying to get a seat before anyone else. If this behavior gets out of hand—especially if you notice other people starting to get hurt (as often happens in the old Musical Chairs game)—you may need to stop all the groups for a moment and challenge them to help each other find creative ways to all sit down safely together during each round of play.

26 SOCK IT TO ME

Using ordinary (but clean) socks, circles of 10–15 people get a chance to experience how good uproarious and sustained laughter feels.

GOALS

To have an experience of juggling cooperatively as a group.

To produce side-splitting, sustained, and uproarious laughter.

To enjoy tossing objects back and forth without worrying about skill levels.

GROUP SIZE

10–15 people per group

TIME FRAME

5–10 minutes

MATERIALS NEEDED

One clean, rolled up athletic knee sock per person (either facilitator- or participant-provided).

PROCESS

1) Have each participant choose a sock and then form small groups of 10–15 people.

2) Each group chooses one of its members to be the "starter" for this exercise.

3) Ask the people in each circle to place their rolled up socks at their starter's feet.

4) Say the following: "In this exercise you will be tossing your socks back and forth to each other. The *first* important objective is for each group to establish a crisscross tossing pattern so that each person has a chance to toss one sock to one other person in the group."

5) Ask each person in the circle to raise a hand in the air. Explain that a person with a raised hand is signaling to the rest of the group that he or she hasn't received a sock yet.

6) The starter in each group then begins the tossing pattern by tossing one sock to a person across the circle. This first person receiving the sock then lowers his or her hand, chooses some other person across the circle with a raised hand, and tosses the sock to that person. This continues until everyone has caught a sock.

   ☞ *It's very important that people keep their hands raised until they have actually received a sock thrown by another person.*

7) When no more hands are raised, the last person holding the sock tosses it back to the starter. By now a unique tossing pattern has been established in which each member of the circle has thrown a sock to one other person in the group and received a sock thrown by another person in the group.

   ☞ *Make sure people remember who they threw to in this initial tossing pattern. If any group is unsure, have them quickly repeat the pattern. This may seem like a complicated beginning, but it really helps ensure that no one is left out of the exercise.*

8) After this tossing pattern has been set up, tell the groups that there is really only one rule in this exercise: "Whenever you find a sock in your hand *for any reason*—receiving it from your designated tosser; catching someone else's toss; *stealing* a sock from your neighbor (?!); or simply retrieving socks on the floor—*whenever*

you have a sock in your hand *always* toss that sock to that same person you tossed to in the initial tossing pattern. But remember that someone else is also tossing to you!"

9) Give the following instructions to the starters:

➤ You will officially begin the activity by tossing one sock to that same person with whom you began the tossing pattern. When that first sock is halfway around the circle, add another sock chosen from the pile at your feet, then another sock and another sock.

➤ Let your group get comfortable juggling 4–5 socks for a minute or so before adding the rest of the socks.

10) When this activity ends, it is helpful to let the groups share their thoughts and feelings about what they have just experienced together. This sharing also allows people to catch their breath, since this activity is definitely one of the more aerobic ones in this book!

VARIATIONS

• Each person holds onto his or her sock, instead of placing it at the feet of the starter. The game then begins when everyone all at once tosses his or her sock to the designated person in the tossing pattern. In this way *all* socks are being tossed and received by everyone right from the beginning of the exercise, creating instant pandemonium.

• Substitute other readily available objects, such as Koosh® balls from your toy collection. But be really careful about the weight of any alternate objects, since many of them can hurt people who aren't watching who is throwing to them.

• Introduce a wider variety of sizes of tossing objects. For instance, add a few inflatable beach balls into the juggling mix.

• Ask people to throw socks with their nondominant hand. This can also help restrain those people who can't resist seeing how hard they can throw a sock to "fake out" another person.

NOTES

- In our culture there is a high level of importance attached, especially with males, to being able to skillfully throw and catch various objects in various ways on various kinds of playing fields, usually under highly competitive conditions. Many children have been thoroughly shamed at an early age by grown-ups and other children for "not being good enough" at throwing and catching. I still remember how awful it felt in junior high when I was chosen last (if at all) for baseball games after school. In some participants, this activity may also trigger a replay of some of these old, mostly negative "tapes" about throwing and catching. These thoughts and feelings could stimulate a useful group discussion.

- Athletic knee socks serve as ideal juggling objects. When rolled up they provide just about the right size and heft for a tossing object—not too hard, not too soft—and are also readily available, easily replaced, and inexpensive. They're sort of like indoor snowballs.

- After this exercise I sometimes ask people if they were thinking or worrying about anything else while they were tossing the socks back and forth. The answer is usually a resounding "No!" This group response can be used to reinforce one of the primary values of play and these sorts of games; namely, that participants are almost forced to live totally and completely in the moment.

- Depending on the group and your own level of mischievousness, you may want to title this exercise "The Joy of Socks."

RESOURCES

Juggling for the Complete Klutz. John Cassidy. This classic, million copy best-seller will help you and people in your groups personally master an important skill all of you may have been secretly wanting to learn ever since your first trip to the circus. Three colorful juggling bags are attached to each book.

© 1993 Whole Person Associates   210 W Michigan   Duluth MN 55802-1908   (218) 727-0500

27 SPOONING

Participants learn how to hang spoons on their noses as a way of confronting and pushing through barriers to becoming more playful.

GOALS

To experience total silliness while also learning a sometimes useful social skill.

To recognize the social pressures and feelings of embarrassment that can get in the way of acting more childlike, playful, and spontaneous.

GROUP SIZE

Unlimited

TIME FRAME

5–10 minutes

MATERIALS NEEDED

One metal teaspoon per person; one paper towel or napkin per person.

PROCESS

1) Give the following instructions:

➤ Use the napkin or paper towel to make sure your spoon is absolutely clean and dry.

➤ Next, rub the napkin or paper towel across your nose to ensure that it is completely free of all moisture, make-up, and oil.

➤ Take the spoon and breathe on the inside of the curved part of the metal bowl.

➤ Gently hang the spoon on the tip of your nose.

VARIATIONS

- See what other activities—such as walking, talking, and chewing gum—people can perform while maintaining the delicate balance needed to keep the spoon in place.

- People who learn this skill right away and become rather easily bored may want to try simultaneously hanging spoons on their foreheads, cheeks, and chins. (It *can* be done!)

- As in all significant new activities, continual practice is very important! Advanced spooning students will naturally look for practice studios more public than workshop meeting rooms. Restaurants are a good place to start, since the management so thoughtfully provides all the necessary materials right at hand. One hundred percent participation from each person around the table helps in these environments. Staff meetings next?

- Persons wishing to maintain the proper amount of personal dignity and social grace during this activity will most likely feel more comfortable with silver or gold-plated spoons. Stainless steel and aluminum are, well, so ordinary.

- It's also important that people who learn how to spoon accept the responsibility of teaching this skill to all of their friends, loved ones, and colleagues.

NOTES

- I first learned this life-changing skill at the evening banquet of a large food service convention in Michigan, where I had earlier that day presented several play workshops. As I entered the conference center ballroom filled with hundreds of people, I just happened to walk up to a table where seven people were at that very moment studiously practicing the fine art of spoon hanging. Being a quick study in most technical matters, I sat right down and soon became a master. Half an hour and much laughter later, we looked around us and found that people at other tables in all directions spreading out from our own were also modeling our behavior and practicing spooning.

• I never tire of watching people learn to spoon. This exercise is a splendid antidote for what C. W. Metcalf calls "terminal professionalism," and—take my word for it—people who lead playful workshops can suffer from this disease as much as any other teacher or facilitator. The first time I hung that spoon on the end of my nose in public I really began to understand how uncomfortable, silly, awkward, and embarrassed people may feel when I ask them to do something playful at one of my workshops. This insight has greatly aided my own work and growth as a facilitator.

© 1993 Whole Person Associates   210 W Michigan   Duluth MN 55802-1908 (218) 727-0500

The end of childhood is when things cease to astonish us.

Eugene Ionesco

WONDERING AROUND

28   KID POCKETS

Participants deliberately cultivate their sense of wonder by walking around and noticing small items that have some significance for them.

GOAL

To experience the childlike quality of wandering around and hunting for various "treasures."

GROUP SIZE

Unlimited

TIME FRAME

20–30 minutes

MATERIALS NEEDED

One small paper bag per person to serve as a pocket.

PROCESS

1) Begin by making the following statement: "For perhaps thousands of years, adult persons have been amazed at the stuff children pick up and put into their pockets, some of which these aforementioned adult persons tend to unexpectedly discover when sorting laundry."

2) Ask the following questions:

   ✔ How many of you can remember some of the neat stuff you picked up as children?

✔ Do any of you know any children who keep some item that is important to them?

✔ Do any of you still have a little box that you like to keep stuff in?

3) Have each participant take a paper bag and go wandering around for a while (like beachcombers) through whatever environment they choose. Outdoors always makes a good choice.

4) Tell participants that if they notice something that really strikes their fancy or fills them with a sense of awe or wonder, to pick it up and put it into their bag.

5) Encourage people to grab things that really amaze them— usually very simple items that the child part of them sees as a real treasure. The purpose of this activity is not to fill up the bag with a lot of random stuff but to choose items that have some significance.

6) When participants come back, ask them to take a few minutes and share with each other at least one of the treasures in their bags.

VARIATIONS

- Have people notice things that can't (or shouldn't) be put in their paper bag (like clouds, bugs, trees, animals, rare art, etc.). Then tell them to write out their thoughts about what they see and to put those "thoughts" into their bags.

NOTES

- As Yogi Berra once said, "Isn't it amazing what you can see if you just look around." This activity helps grown-ups relearn what children do continuously and naturally.

- This activity can also be easily integrated into a lunch period or break, since people automatically wander off from the meeting space at these times.

- I once read a story about a therapist who found himself increasingly frustrated with a patient's lack of progress and tendency to "stay in his head" a lot. In the middle of one session, as his patient talked on and on in the same old way, the therapist suddenly blurted out, "Go outside and look at the bark of ten trees!" In shock, the patient stopped talking and, to his therapist's amazement, left the room. Two hours later the man came back smiling and transformed, because he really *had* gone out and looked at the bark of ten trees! As he looked, he truly became filled with wonder at the differences he saw. And as he began to open himself to this kind of awareness, he made progress in his therapy.

This activity is not meant to be therapy, but for some people just taking this small amount of time to go playfully wandering around is highly therapeutic. Many of us, like the man in the story, have also learned to deal with life mostly through our heads. We become so used to making time only for the necessary and practical matters in our lives that we seldom allow ourselves to just "wonder around" in amazement at what washes up on our various shores.

29   RACCOON HANDS

In this activity participants explore their environment using the senses of another creature.

GOALS

To explore the surrounding environment with a slightly altered set of tools (hands).

To notice which human skills and senses people take for granted.

To better appreciate the senses and strengths of different animals and the valuable lessons people can learn from them.

GROUP SIZE

Unlimited

TIME FRAME

10 minutes

MATERIALS NEEDED

Rolls of 2-inch-wide masking or adhesive tape (no duct tape, please!).

PROCESS

1) Have participants place their thumbs in the palms of their hands.

2) Tell them to help each other place a piece of tape over their thumbs and palms and around the backs of both hands, completely immobilizing the thumbs of both hands.

3) Have each person then wander around the room, exploring the environment as "humans without thumbs." Tell them to go

© 1993 Whole Person Associates   210 W Michigan   Duluth MN 55802-1908   (218) 727-0500

through as many ordinary motions and activities as possible, such as picking up water glasses, opening doors, etc.

4) After 3–4 minutes of this activity, have people stop and close their eyes.

5) Say the following: "Get a clear picture of a raccoon you have seen or met sometime in your life. Imagine for the next few minutes that you are not a human, but rather a raccoon exploring this environment. Focus on what is important to you and what you are looking for."

6) After 2–3 minutes of raccoon exploration, ask participants to get together in small groups of 4–5 people and share what they experienced. (Have people keep the tape on their hands during this sharing.) Ask the following questions for discussion:

   ✔ What was it like being a four-fingered human? What did you notice? What did you find most frustrating?

   ✔ Besides our opposable thumbs, what other senses and built-in tools do humans take for granted?

   ✔ What did you learn as a raccoon? What had value for you?

   ✔ What did you look for as you explored? What was missing in the room from the raccoon point of view?"

7) When time is up, ask people to carefully assist each other in removing the tape from their hands.

VARIATIONS

• Eliminate the tape and have people consciously hold their thumbs in their palms (but the experience is not quite as powerful this way).

• Choose another animal that has significance for people in terms of the different or heightened senses well beyond humans.

• Have participants share in small groups of 4–5 people what kinds of animals they would like to be for a day or two—and especially *why* they want to be those animals.

NOTES

- Raccoons, along with otters and dolphins, are some of the animals who most remind me of what curiosity and play look like. Raccoons are always turning over every loose thing to see what's underneath.

- Not really so long ago most humans knew how to live in harmony with all of life, especially with animals. Most native peoples haven't forgotten how to appreciate the many important lessons other creatures can teach us. Native American stories about the "people" of one kind or another, such as the *Bear* people, the *Hawk* people, the *Mouse* people, the *Snake* people, and, of course, the *Human* people, show how they honor all living beings and point out that we can all appreciate and learn valuable lessons from these "others" we find in our homes and on our planet.

RESOURCES

Bat Conservation International. Humans have misunderstood and feared bats (along with spiders, snakes, wolves, and a host of other creatures) for millennia. This organization educates people about the essential, often surprising role bats play in the life of our world. For more information about publications, products, and membership, contact: Bat Conservation International, P.O. Box 162603, Austin, TX 78716.

Delta Society. The Delta Society is an international clearinghouse of information about the positive interaction of people, animals, and the environment. For membership and other information, contact: The Delta Society, P.O. Box 1080, Renton, WA 98057-1080. 206/226-7357.

Gorilla Foundation. Koko and Michael are two lowland gorillas who have learned to use sign language to communicate with humans. (Koko is also the gorilla who adopted a cat for a pet!) The words "astonishing" and "inspiring" are too mild to describe the discoveries being made as humans and gorillas speak with each other. Active membership is only $25 a year, and helps support continuing face-to-face interspecies communication. For more information, contact: The Gorilla Foundation, P.O. Box 620530, Woodside, CA 94062. 415/851-8505.

In the Shadow of a Rainbow: The True Story of a Friendship Between Man & Wolf. Robert Franklin Leslie.

International Wolf Center. The center's goal is research and public education about the wolf and related species. For information about membership, contact: International Wolf Center, c/o Vermilion Community College, 1900 East Camp Street, Ely, MN 55731. 218/365-3256.

Kinship With All Life. J. Allen Boone.

Medicine Cards. Jamie Sams and David Carson. Illustrations by Angela Werneke. These cards (and the accompanying book) will help you tap into the strength and character of various animals as a source of insight, understanding, and personal power. "The medicine referred to . . . is anything that improves one's connection to the Great Mystery and to all life." Available in bookstores, or by contacting: Bear & Company, P.O. Drawer 2860, Santa Fe, NM 87504-2860. 505/983-5968.

The Four Footed Therapist: How Your Pet Can Help You Solve Your Problems. Janet Ruckert.

The Once & Future King. The Book of Merlin. T. H. White. In these two classic books about the life of King Arthur, the wizard Merlin transforms the young (and later the old) Arthur into other creatures so that Arthur can better understand the strengths, differences, and limitations of those other worlds.

The View from the Oak: The Private Worlds of Other Creatures. Judith and Herbert Kohl.

To Whom It May Concern: An Investigation of the Art of Elephants. David Gucwa and James Ehmann. (Out of print, but fascinating reading.)

30   READ US A STORY

Participants get back in touch with the gentle simplicity, beauty, and truth of children's books as they read to each other in small groups or are read to in one large group.

GOALS

To become aware of the magic, power, and truth often found in children's stories.

To experience the delight of being read to.

GROUP SIZE

10–15 people per group

TIME FRAME

10–20 minutes

MATERIALS NEEDED

Your own and other people's favorite children's books and stories.

PROCESS

1) Have participants share with each other or the whole group the title of at least one of their favorite stories or books from childhood, especially ones grown-ups read to them. Ask them to say why these books were so special and how they felt when someone read to them.

2) Ask participants if they would like you to read them a story. (The answer is almost always an enthusiastic "Yes!")

3) Gather participants around you so that everyone can easily hear your voice and see any illustrations in the book you will be reading. If the room is carpeted, participants may enjoy lying or sitting down on the floor.

4) Read at least one story to the group, allowing plenty of time for everyone to see the pictures in an illustrated book.

5) If the group is larger than 15 people, you may want to read a story that relies less on illustrations and more on people's own imaginations.

6) After you finish reading the story, have participants share something they felt, thought, or remembered during the reading.

VARIATIONS

- Have a few participants bring in their favorite children's book to share with the group.

- If you have enough children's books to go around, have participants form small groups of 4–6 people and take turns reading and sharing a book in their small group.

- Make up and tell your own story.

NOTES

- This can be a great activity to use after lunch or anytime when people are feeling sleepy and mellow. It also works well as a quiet interlude sandwiched between other more active games and activities.

- One day in the children's section of one of my favorite bookstores, I found an especially delicious new book, and quickly settled down onto the only grown-up-sized chair I could find in the area. As happens with these books, I instantly got caught up in the magical blend of words and pictures. Somewhere in the middle of the story I happened to look up and noticed that right there beside me sat a small boy on a tiny chair, his own nose also pasted to the pages of a book he had found. Many years of time separated that little boy and me, but there was no distance or difference at all between the spirits who turned the pages of those books.

- For a long time, probably since I was a child, I have intuitively evaluated stories and books in a very simple way. Do I get shivers of delight and excitement as I read or as I hear the story being read or told? Am I inspired to stretch beyond my normal dimensions and boundaries? Are new possibilities, insights, and truths awakened in me? Stories that affect me in these ways are the ones I return to over and over again. Why? Because they nourish and reconnect me with my whole self. I therefore don't really care at all whether some "expert" or "authority" has labeled a book or story "science fiction," "fantasy," "children's book," or "literature." Is it that way for you, too?

RESOURCES

I recommend that you regularly spend time browsing in and borrowing from the children's book section of your local library. You may get so charmed by this process of getting back in touch with the power and wisdom of children's literature that you will also want to start your own collection.

Storytelling

Creative Storytelling: Choosing, Inventing & Sharing Tales for Children. Jack Maguire.

Don't Tell the Grown-ups: Why Kids Love the Books They Do. Alison Lurie.

In the Ever After: Fairy Tales & the Second Half of Life. Allan B. Chinen.

My Voice Will Go with You: The Teaching Tales of Milton H. Erikson. Sidney Rosen, editor.

© 1993 Whole Person Associates   210 W Michigan   Duluth MN 55802-1908   (218) 727-0500

National Association for the Preservation and Perpetuation of Storytelling. For information about publications, membership, and other services, contact: NAPPS, P.O. Box 309, Jonesborough, TN 37659. 615/753-2171.

Pipers at the Gates of Dawn: The Wisdom of Children's Literature. Jonathan Cott.

The Boy Who Would Be a Helicopter: The Uses of Storytelling in the Classroom. Vivian Gussin Paley.

The Language of the Night: Essays on Fantasy and Science Fiction. Ursula K. Le Guin. Includes a most insightful essay titled "Why Are Americans Afraid of Dragons?"

"The Story-Telling Animal." Kathryn Morton. *New York Times Book Review* (89:1+, Dec 23, 1985).

The Uses of Enchantment: The Meaning & Importance of Fairy Tales. Bruno Bettelheim.

The Way of the Storyteller. Ruth Sawyer.

Stories

Any book written by Byrd Baylor and illustrated by Peter Parnall, including *Hawk, I'm Your Brother; Everybody Needs a Rock; The Way to Start a Day;* and *I'm in Charge of Celebrations.*

Badger's Parting Gifts. Susan Varley.

Caretakers of Wonder. Cooper Edens.

Dandelion Wine. Ray Bradbury. (A genuinely magical book, especially the chapters about getting new sneakers, the "time machine," great-grandma's passing; and grandma's cooking.)

Guess Who My Favorite Person Is. Byrd Baylor. Illustrations by Robert Andrew Parker.

If You're Afraid of the Dark, Remember the Night Rainbow. Cooper Edens.

Ming Lo Moves the Mountain. Arnold Lobel.

Nimby. Jasper Tomkins.

Old Turtle. Douglas Wood. Illustratrations by Cheng-Khee Chee.

Rosie & Michael. Judith Viorst. Illustrations by Lorna Tomei.

Stone Soup. Ann McGovern. Illustrations by Winslow Pels.

The Catalog. Jasper Tomkins.

The Giving Tree. Shel Silverstein.

The House at Pooh Corner. A. A. Milne. Decorations by Ernest H. Shepard.

The Little Prince. Antoine de Saint Exupéry.

The Sky Jumps Into Your Shoes at Night. Jasper Tomkins.

The Story of Ferdinand. Munro Leaf. Illustrations by Robert Lawson.

The Velveteen Rabbit: Or How Toys Become Real. Margery Williams. Illustrations by William Nicholson.

There's a Nightmare in My Closet. Mercer Mayer.

There's No Such Place As Far Away. Richard Bach. Paintings by H. Lee Shapiro.

Where the Sidewalk Ends. Shel Silverstein.

Where the Wild Things Are. Maurice Sendak.

Who Speaks for Wolf: A Native American Learning Story. Paula Underwood. Art by Frank Howell. A beautifully told and illustrated story of one people's struggle to live peacefully within their environment as they learn valuable lessons from nature, circumstances, and each other. A companion teacher's guide titled *Three Strands in the Braid: A Guide for Enablers of Learning* is also available. Exceptionally relevant in classrooms of all kinds, including K-12, college, and organizational training. To order these books, contact: A Tribe of Two Press, P.O. Box 216, San Anselmo, CA 94979. 415/457-6548.

© 1993 Whole Person Associates   210 W Michigan   Duluth MN 55802-1908   (218) 727-0500

31   THE FIRST TIME EVER

As a way of stimulating awareness, participants are asked to keep journals about the many different things around and within them that they notice or see for the first time.

GOAL

To develop a habit of noticing all kinds of things about the world the way children do—for the first time.

GROUP SIZE

Unlimited

TIME FRAME

10–15 minutes

MATERIALS NEEDED

Small notebooks for participants to carry with them.

PROCESS

1) Ask how many participants can remember being around infants or small children.

2) Have them share what it's like being around these small ones who are experiencing almost everything for the very first time.

3) Have the group briefly discuss why they think so many adults seem to lose their ability to see the world through fresh eyes.

4) Ask for suggestions about how people might regain some of that "wondering around" ability they had as children.

5) As a "homework" assignment to address this problem, ask people to begin keeping journals of their FTE (First Time Ever) experiences, writing down what and when and where they have seen or noticed something for the very first time.

6) At the next workshop session, have people share some of their FTE discoveries with each other.

VARIATIONS

• If your group is only meeting once, have participants spend 10–15 minutes looking for or thinking about FTE's, writing them in their notebooks, and then sharing them with the group.

NOTES

• The physicist John Wheeler once was asked what advice he would give young people. He answered, "Find the strangest thing, and then explore it!" I think each one of us regularly needs to be encouraged (in the words of the Starship Enterprise's mission statement) ". . . to explore strange new worlds, to seek out new life and new civilizations, to boldly go where no one has gone before." This activity is intended to help people stay more creative, successful, and happy by limbering up their natural abilities to see the world anew.

• Here are some of my favorite FTEs:

One day as I walked in to pick up my mail at the post office—something I have done hundreds of times before—I heard a strange noise, looked up, and saw a woman buying stamps with a parrot on her shoulder.

One time while driving I found myself staring at a large "Student Driver" sign on the back of an 18 wheeler semi-truck rig in front of me.

Once on a long trip I exited off a freeway to find something to eat. At the bottom of the exit ramp, a car had pulled well off the road onto a grassy area, and both the driver and passenger doors of the car were standing wide-open. Two people, a man and a woman, were standing on either side of the car and having what looked like a pretty heated argument with each other, in sign language!

One summer evening in New Mexico, I joined hundreds of people in an amphitheater overlooking the entrance to Carlsbad Caverns. As darkness fell we listened to the rangers tell us about the hundreds of thousands of small female brown bats who raise their babies inside the cave. Soon the bats themselves began flying out of the cave, going off into the night to provide for their families by feeding on huge quantities of insects. Much later, after most people had left, I stood there with another visitor and the two rangers, still watching thousands of these tiny bats spiral up into the darkness. As I listened, I heard a soft murmuring sound, which I thought was a river flowing deep in the cave. When I asked the rangers about it, they said, "No, it's the sound of bat wings."

RESOURCES

A Natural History of the Senses. Diane Ackerman.

A Sand County Almanac. Aldo Leopold.

All I Really Need To Know I Learned In Kindergarten. Robert Fulghum.

Dymaxion™ Sky-Ocean World Map. Buckminster Fuller. "Shows our planet as . . . a one-world island in a one-world ocean, without any visible distortion of the relative shape and sizes of the land and sea . . . An essential tool for learning about Spaceship Earth and the environment." For a catalog about this and other awareness-altering products, contact: Buckminster Fuller Institute. 1743 South La Cienega Blvd, Los Angeles, CA 90035. 213/837-7710.

Everybody Needs a Rock. Byrd Baylor. Illustrations by Peter Parnall.

How Real Is Real? Paul Watzlawick.

I'm in Charge of Celebrations. Byrd Baylor. Illustrations by Peter Parnall.

Mister God, This is Anna. Fynn.

Pilgrim at Tinker Creek. Annie Dillard.

Playful Perception: Choosing How to Experience Your World. Herbert Leff.

Powers of Ten: About the Relative Size of Things in the Universe. Charles and Ray Eames.

Powers of Ten. Charles and Ray Eames. An extraordinary film from Pyramid Films, based on the book. Call 800/523-0118 for a copy of their latest film and video catalog.

The Immense Journey. Loren Eiseley.

The Lives of a Cell. Lewis Thomas.

The Singing Creek Where the Willows Grow: The Rediscovered Diary of Opal Whiteley. Presented by Benjamin Hoff.

The View from the Oak: The Private Worlds of Other Creatures. Judith and Herbert Kohl.

The Way to Start a Day. Byrd Baylor. Illustrations by Peter Parnall.

Turnabout Map™ of the Americas. Why do we always assume North has to be "on top" on maps? This geographically correct map of North and South America will dramatically alter your perception by turning your accustomed world upside down and creating a new world of understanding. Available from: Laguna Sales, 7040 Via Valverde, San Jose, CA 95135.

32 STORY CIRCLES

In small groups participants rekindle their imaginations and the positive power of fantasy by making up stories together.

GOALS

To rediscover the delight of "making stuff up."

To experience fun, whimsy, imagination, and wonder.

GROUP SIZE

5–6 people per group

TIME FRAME

10–15 minutes

MATERIALS NEEDED

None

PROCESS

1) Form small groups of 5–6 people and say the following:

➤ I am going to begin a story and would like you all to continue it (in different ways, of course) in your small groups.

➤ When I reach the end of *my* beginning of the story, I will simply say, "What happened next was . . ." and then one person in each group will continue making up the story for 30 seconds to a minute. He or she will then pause, turn to the next person in the group, and say, "What happened next was . . ." The next person then takes up the story where it left off and so on.

➤ Each small group will probably have a chance to go around the circle two or three times in the time allotted. If anyone can't think of "what happened next . . ." just say, "Right now, I'm unable to remember what happened next, but . . ." Turn to the next person and say, "I think she (or he) remembers."

2) Begin the activity with the following story or make up one of your own. Be as vivid as possible in your descriptions.

Once in a land not so far away, in a time not so long ago, a small band of travelers followed a dusty trail across a hot, dry desert. For days and days they could barely find water, food, or shade. Their only hope of survival was to reach the range of mountains they saw on the horizon. They knew they would find rest and refreshment there. And maybe new adventures, if they could just get to those distant green hills.

After much effort they finally arrived. All of them gazed with wonder and excitement at the lofty peaks they had watched from a distance for so long. Two days later, as they climbed halfway up the tallest mountain, they discovered a very large and ancient rock. Now, of course, mountains are made of very large rocks and most rocks are ancient, but this particular rock was special. It looked like one of the first rocks ever made, and right away everyone noticed a really big opening at the base of the rock.

The travelers drew closer to the rock and peered down into the hole.

What happened next was . . .

VARIATIONS

• When time has run out, have each group briefly share with the others the last 15–20 seconds of their stories to highlight the amazing variety in imagination creatively expressed during the activity.

- Ursula K. Le Guin once said that a story does not have to be factual in order to be true. Ask participants what they learned about themselves, each other, and the worlds they just created in their stories.

- Collect postcards and magazine clippings of interesting, thought-provoking scenes (outdoors, people, animals, workplaces, etc.). Have one person from each group choose a picture that "speaks" to him or her. That person then begins telling a story to their small groups based on what she or he sees in that picture. Once started, the story is passed around the circle in the same way as above. This is a bit more challenging than beginning each group with the same story, but with the right groups it can be a lot of fun. (If you laminate the pictures with plastic, they will last indefinitely.)

NOTES

- Someone once told me that children are born with an advanced degree, something called the M.S.U. Degree. This is their degree in *making stuff up*. This activity definitely helps rekindle the imagination and wonder in grown-up people.

- People's faces as they sit in these story circles are like those of children gathered around small campfires. Years seem to melt away, eyes get very wide and intent, and people often stay very still as they eagerly lean forward into the story worlds they are creating together.

RESOURCES

See storytelling resources listed under **Read Us a Story.**

The song "Once Upon A Time" by Michael Martin Murphy (from his *Americana* album) is a beautiful reminder of how stories can reconnect us with ourselves and with each other.

33 THE TOY BOX

In this highly experiential activity, participants spontaneously explore and play with the contents of a box of toys.

GOAL

To experience a period of unstructured free play and exploration, individually and with others.

GROUP SIZE

Depends on the size of the facilitator's toy collection. Unlimited, if participants bring in their own toys.

TIME FRAME

15–20 minutes

MATERIALS NEEDED

A box or bag filled with toys (see **Notes** below). Toys brought in by participants (optional).

PROCESS

1) Have participants share their answers to the following questions in one large group, in pairs, or in small groups.

   ✔ How many of you can remember a favorite toy you played with as a child?

   ✔ What was so special about that toy?

   ✔ How did you feel when you were playing with it?

2) Tell participants that you have brought along your very own marvelous toy collection to share with them.

3) Before opening the box of toys, ask participants to play safe. Being blindsided by a flying disc or ball is not pleasant for anyone.

4) Open the box and just let people spontaneously explore and play with the toys for the rest of the time period.

5) Keep groups to around 20–25 people so that each participant feels part of a "playground" they know.

VARIATIONS

- At the end of the play period, have people hold onto one toy they found particularly significant. Then have them share with each other in small groups or with the whole group why that toy is important to them and what they discovered or experienced while playing with it.

- If you can let people know ahead of time, have them bring in one of their favorite toys to share with others during the play time.

- I remember one young man whose eyes lit up when he said, "Can I dump the box out?" Dumping the toy box out onto the floor is a great way for one or two people to begin the activity. If you let this happen, however, make sure you have removed fragile items ahead of time.

- Have people each bring in a wrapped toy that costs less than $5. Then have a "toy exchange" where each person picks a toy other than the one they brought with them to the workshop. (Do this while the toys are still wrapped!)

- Encourage people to find one special toy they can carry with them everywhere they go during the day, both as a symbol of play and as something they really can play with when they need a creative break. Also, have people think of creative phrases they can have ready when adults openly criticize them for playing or when their own inner adult voice starts in on them.

NOTES

• Ask a few people to help you pack up your toys at the end of the activity or the whole session. This can help avoid a common facilitator experience, sometimes known as the everyone-has-gone-home-and-left-me-with-this-mess-to-clean-up syndrome.

• Depending on your budget, stock your box with toys that are not only versatile and useful for play with individuals and groups but that also touch you in some way. Each time I do a workshop I usually hear about at least one terrific new toy I didn't know existed, and it's usually not too long before I add it to my collection!

• The contents of my own toy box have been steadily expanding over the past few years and currently include:

Koosh® Balls (many different texture, sizes, and varieties); juggling bags (formerly attached to my copy of *Juggling for the Complete Klutz*); plastic juggling pins; jump ropes (short ones for individuals and long ones for groups); Silly Putty®; Aerobie® flying rings and boomerangs (outside use only); Foxtails™ (careful indoor use); Frisbees®; jacks; marbles (regular and magnetic); Whoosh® flying rings; bubbles (especially a Bubble Bear™); brightly colored scarves and handkerchiefs; Grip Ball™ velcro catch set (tennis balls that stick to velcro mitts); Monster and Regular size Balzac™ balloon balls (plus extra 11- and 15-inch-diameter latex balloons); Slinky™ (metal not plastic); paddle ball; Wheel-O™; hula hoops (the collapsible kind are ideal for trainers and teachers); surplus parachute; teddy bear; 50–60 rolled up knee socks; magic wands; yo-yos; kaleidoscopes; yellow plastic cones (for boundary markers); and small puzzles.

• Most grown-ups are careful when playing. But make sure you deal ahead of time with any attachment you have to any of your toys. If you absolutely do not want a toy broken, lost, or misused in some way, leave it out of the toy box you share at workshops.

© 1993 Whole Person Associates   210 W Michigan   Duluth MN 55802-1908   (218) 727-0500

RESOURCES

Animal Town Cooperative Ventures publishes a wonderful catalog of cooperative and noncompetitive games, toys, books, and puzzles. Contact: Animal Town Cooperative Ventures, P.O. Box 485, Healdsburg, CA 95448. 800/445-8642.

Flying Apparatus Catalog. This essential toy source contains most Klutz Press toy publications—including the famous *Juggling for the Complete Klutz*—plus an abundance of other playful items such as unicycles. Free from: Klutz Press, 2121 Staunton Court, Palo Alto, CA 94306. 415/424-0739. I double dare you not to laugh just *reading* this catalog!

Hearthsong—A Catalog for Families. A delightful collection of books, toys, and craft materials for children of all ages. 800/325-2502.

Into the Wind. Call 800/541-0314 for a copy of their latest kite catalog.

The Nature Company offers a wide variety of toys and other wonders. Call 800/227-1114 and request their free catalog.

Project Adventure provides another excellent source for toys and props (including collapsible plastic hoops) in their *Project Adventure Equipment Catalog.* Contact: Project Adventure, P.O. Box 100, Hamilton, MA 01936. 508/468-7981.

34 WHAT'S THE POINT?

Looking at a simple black dot, participants are asked to come up with as many explanations and possibilities as they can of what that dot "really is."

GOAL

To stretch people's imaginations beyond "normal" boundaries and limitations.

GROUP SIZE

Unlimited, in groups of 4–5 people

TIME FRAME

5–10 minutes

MATERIALS NEEDED

Flipchart and markers or blackboard and chalk (optional); overhead projector (optional); **What's the Point?** worksheet (optional as as overhead transparency).

PROCESS

1) Have participants form small groups of 4–5 people, then share the following story:

> *There once was a woman who kept two goldfish in a small glass bowl. One day when she was getting ready to clean the bowl, she decided to give her fish an extra treat. Instead of putting them into a small dish while she cleaned their bowl, she drew the bathtub full of water and placed them in it, thinking they would enjoy the extra freedom for a little while.*

*But when she came back an hour later, the fish were swim-
ming round and round in a small circle* exactly *the same size
as the small glass bowl in which they normally lived.*

2) Say the following: "Humans aren't goldfish. But how many of
us get used to perceiving the world in certain predictable ways
and forget that the boundaries we see around us are very often the
ones we put there?"

3) As a simple demonstration of this fact, ask people to cross their
arms, noting which arm is on top. Then ask them to reverse the
way their arms are crossed.

4) Ask them how that feels. For many people the second way feels
almost completely "unnatural."

5) Hand out a **What's the Point?** worksheet to each small group.
Ask the people in each group to write down on that sheet, or on
a separate piece of paper, all of the different things that circular
mark might really be. Have the group generate as many alterna-
tives as they can in the next 4–5 minutes.

6) If there is time, let the small groups share some of their answers
with the whole group to get a sense of the many possibilities
people saw.

VARIATIONS

• Project the worksheet as an overhead transparency—or simply
draw it on a flipchart or blackboard—and have the whole group
work together to generate possibilities.

NOTES

• Some adults have a tough time with this assignment. If people
have trouble coming up with a lot of possibilities, suggest they
consciously try looking at the possibilities the way a five-year-
old might see them. For children it's usually a lot easier because

they don't have a lot of preconceptions about what something is or isn't, and can most of the time access their imaginations much more freely.

* I suggest that you as the facilitator sit down before the workshop and exercise your own imagination with this worksheet. For example, the dot on the paper could be a dog's nose or a black hole or the skin of a Dalmatian or a total eclipse of the sun or the period at the end of this sentence or a black eye or a lump of coal in a snowstorm or—well, you get the idea.

RESOURCES

See listings under **The First Time Ever** activity for resources that can help people expand the boundaries of what they think is possible.

© 1993 Whole Person Associates   210 W Michigan   Duluth MN 55802-1908   (218) 727-0500

I know of no other manner of dealing with great tasks, then as play.

Albert Schweitzer

TAKING IT HOME

35 BUMPER STICKERS (p 140)

Participants invent or recall phrases that will help them remember to laugh and play more. (5–10 minutes)

36 LETTER FROM CAMP (p 142)

This powerful activity allows participants an opportunity to reflect on what they have most enjoyed and learned during the workshop by writing a letter home to their "inner" parents. (10–15 minutes)

37 MOOMBA (p 145)

Participants are introduced to a magic word they can use as a way of reminding themselves of the need to laugh and play and lighten up more. (5 minutes)

38 OFFICIAL MEMBERSHIP CARD (p 149)

Every person coming to the workshop automatically becomes a lifetime member in the Society of Childlike Grown-ups, and receives a membership card to prove it. (3–5 minutes)

39 SQUISHER (p 153)

Participants use balloons, sand, and colored markers to playfully create a physical object they can take with them as a reminder of the need to honor the child within. (10–15 minutes)

40 THE LAUGHING PLACE (p 155)

Using crayons and markers, participants draw pictures that show what it takes to create a place where laughter and play are found and experienced more often, both on and off the job. (10–15 minutes)

35   BUMPER STICKERS

Participants invent or recall phrases that will help them remember to laugh and play more.

GOAL

To exercise the imagination in coming up with positive and playful phrases that encourage more childlike behavior and attitudes in grown-ups.

GROUP SIZE

Unlimited

TIME FRAME

5–10 minutes

MATERIALS NEEDED

One 8 ½ x 11 inch sheet of white paper per person; watercolor markers in various colors.

PROCESS

1) Have participants fold their blank sheets of paper into thirds length-wise, carefully crease the paper along the folds, and tear them into three separate strips.

2) Have people think of positive "bumper sticker" phrases that somehow capture the need for grown-ups to be more childlike and playful, to lighten up and laugh more often. As examples you could mention such phrases as *It's Never Too Late to Have a Happy Childhood; You're Never Too Old for Recess; Growing Up is Hard Work—Once You've Grown Up, the Hard Work is Optional;* or that wonderful phrase from one of Nintendo's® ads,

Have You Had Your Fun Today? People may also want to write actual bumper stickers they have seen while driving.

3) Inform participants that really effective bumper stickers get their important messages across in as few words as possible, are easy to read quickly and safely while driving, and often use humor to get people's attention.

4) Allow a few minutes for everyone to create at least one bumper sticker with the paper and markers.

5) Have people attach rolled-up loops of masking tape to the back of their bumper stickers and then get help sticking their bumper stickers onto their backs.

6) Have everyone walk around for a few minutes reading each other's stickers.

VARIATIONS

• If you do this activity early enough in a workshop, have people take off their stickers and stick them on a wall for everyone to see during the rest of the session. Some people may want to write down their favorites.

• Have people keep a notebook in which they write down some of the positive and funny bumper stickers they see as they drive around in their cars each day. Just reading over this list will brighten anyone's gloomy day.

NOTES

• Doing this activity ahead of time can also add some more interest, excitement, and amusement to the **Rush Hour** activity. With bumper stickers already taped to the shoulders of "cars" or "drivers" in that activity, all the drivers moving around the room will be able to read the other "bumpers." You may find that some participants, feeling particularly brave or smart-alecky, will put their bumper stickers on their behinds instead of their shoulders.

36   LETTER FROM CAMP

This powerful activity allows participants an opportunity to reflect on what they have most enjoyed and learned during the workshop by writing a letter home to their "inner" parents.

GOALS

To reflect on the experience of laughing and playing, and consider ways to stimulate more of this beneficial behavior.

To visually and physically reinforce more direct communication with the child self inside people.

To establish better communication between the "inner child" and the "inner parent."

GROUP SIZE

Unlimited

TIME FRAME

10–15 minutes

MATERIALS NEEDED

One envelope and sheet of lined white paper per person; one pen or soft lead #2 pencil (if possible) per person; one sheet of lined newsprint paper from a Big Chief™ school pad (optional).

PROCESS

1) Have people quietly think about where they are right now. Have them think about how they are feeling, what some of their favorite experiences were during the workshop, what insights

they have had about themselves while laughing and playing, what childlike activities they are planning to introduce into their lives as a result of what they have shared together at the workshop.

2) Have them reflect for a moment on the fact that a workshop filled with an abundance of laughter and play-stimulating activities is really sort of like being at a "summer camp for your inner child."

3) Give the following instructions:

➤ Using your nondominant hand (if you're right-handed, use your left hand, and vice versa), have your "inner child" write a letter home to your "inner parents." Talk about anything you want, including what games you've played, new friends you've made, what the food and camp counselors are like, what neat stuff you've discovered while hiking, how you are feeling, where you want to go and what you want to do with your "parents" when you get home, and so on.

➤ When you have finished writing, fold up your letter and seal it in an envelope. Address the envelope to "(*your name*)'s Inner Parents.

➤ Take the letter home with you, and open it in 2–3 days.

VARIATIONS

• Tell people that after they open their "letters from camp" at home to then have their "inner parents" (using the dominant hand) write a letter back to the inner child as a way of showing they have heard the child. The inner parents should talk about the activities they definitely want to share together with the child. In some cases people may also want to have their inner parents apologize to the inner child for being too busy to play and how that is going to change.

• Have people make up names for the "camps" they are attending as they write their letters home.

© 1993 Whole Person Associates   210 W Michigan   Duluth MN 55802-1908   (218)727-0500

NOTES

- The "inner adult" inside each of us can play a significant role in allowing us to feel OK about playing more often in healthy ways—even when our homework or chores aren't all done (and, of course, even as grown-ups our "homework" and chores never *are* all done).

- Letters created with the nondominant hand very often look like they've been written by first or second graders. This is one of the great powers of this particular writing activity, the way it helps reestablish in a simple, childlike way more direct connection between the adult and child selves inside each person.

- Using the #2 pencil and the lined newsprint paper physically and visually reinforces the link back to childhood and the child self.

- This activity is best done towards the end of a workshop or play session because it builds on what people have experienced together and inside themselves and creates an opportunity to process a variety of very powerful and sometimes conflicting feelings.

- This letter is meant only for the person writing it, unless a person chooses to share it with others.

- By encouraging people to open their letters later at home, this activity automatically creates a valuable way for people to reinforce the insights and activities they shared at the workshop.

RESOURCES

The Power of Your Other Hand. Lucia Cappachione.

37   MOOMBA

Participants are introduced to a magic word they can use as a way of reminding themselves of the need to laugh and play and lighten up more.

GOAL

To think of new ways to laugh, play, and have more fun.

GROUP SIZE

Unlimited

TIME FRAME

5 minutes

MATERIALS NEEDED

One 12-inch-long piece of brightly colored yarn (red, blue, yellow, green, etc.) for each participant; **Moomba** worksheet (optional as an overhead transparency).

PROCESS

1) Make sure each person in the group has a piece of yarn.

2) Write the word *MOOMBA* on a flipchart or blackboard, or display it on an overhead projector.

3) Have people repeat MOOMBA several times, louder each time they say it. Have them place their hand on their chest as they say the word to feel the resonance created.

4) Ask participants what they think MOOMBA means. Then say the following, "In the language of the Australian aboriginal

peoples, MOOMBA means—loosely translated—'Let's get together and have some fun!' "

5) Ask participants to think of at least one new way they are going
to bring more laughter, play, and fun into their lives. Have them
picture what that new activity looks and feels like, and to see
themselves doing it regularly.

6) Have everyone in the group hold up a piece of yarn. Say the
following: "What you are holding in your hands is no ordinary
piece of yarn. It's a MOOMBA string! Like tying a string around
your finger to remember something, the purpose of the MOOMBA
string is to help all of us remember what we are going to do to
include more regular doses of humor, laughter, and play in our
busy lives."

7) Have participants help each other tie a MOOMBA string to their
wrists.

   ☞ *Be sure to get one tied to your wrist as well.*

8) Ask people to proudly wear their MOOMBA strings for as long
as they wish, as a reminder of the human need to have fun.

   ☞ *Even if people remove their MOOMBA strings immediately
   after this activity, they will still feel it around their wrists
   for a while, a simple reminder to laugh and play more.*

VARIATIONS

- Before explaining what MOOMBA means, just put the word up
on the flipchart, blackboard, or overhead projector. Then ask
people in small groups to figure out what the initials might stand
for, as an acronym for our need to include more humor, laughter,
and play in our lives. Then have people share their ideas with the
whole group. (See **Notes** for an interesting acronym one group
suggested to me.)

- As participants are tying the MOOMBA strings onto each
other's wrists, they might want to share with each other what they

have decided to do to stimulate more humor, laughter, and play into their lives. You could also have people wander around for a minute sharing these ideas and plans with a few more of their neighbors.

- Have people raise their arms with the yarn tied on and together shout louder and louder, "Moomba, Moomba, Moomba!"

- Forget the actual pieces of yarn, but make sure the word MOOMBA is firmly anchored—as it will be—in people's minds. It's pretty much an unforgettable word.

NOTES

- At one workshop session, I wrote MOOMBA on the board but forgot to explain its meaning. At the next session with the same group, I finally explained what it meant. At the break a few participants came up to me and said, "Oh, that's what it means." I asked them what they thought it meant. They had decided that M.O.O.M.B.A. was an acronym for My Only Obstacle Must Be Attitude. Amazing! I told them their acronym was the right answer, too.

- Once you introduce this word to some groups, be prepared for it to take on a life of its own as a kind of magical code word for playfulness. The day after I shared this word during my presentation at a summer wellness conference, a person told me that pasted on the inside of all the toilet stalls in one of the dorms was a sheet of paper with the following message: "If you hear someone in the shower and are about to flush, yell MOOMBA!"

© 1993 Whole Person Associates   210 W Michigan   Duluth MN 55802-1908   (218) 727-0500

M	
O	
O	
M	
B	
A	

38 OFFICIAL MEMBERSHIP CARD

Every person coming to the workshop automatically becomes a lifetime member in the Society of Childlike Grown-ups, and receives a membership card to prove it.

GOALS

To give participants a playful souvenir of the workshop.

To offer people a tangible and visible symbol of their absolute, lifetime right to play, a reminder they can carry with them all the time.

GROUP SIZE

Unlimited

TIME FRAME

3–5 minutes

MATERIALS NEEDED

One **Official Membership Card** (photocopied or printed and cut into individual 2 x3 ½inch cards) per person—overhead transparency (optional).

PROCESS

1) Ask participants if they have ever wanted an **Official Membership Card.**

2) Pass out the individual membership cards. Take a minute for people to write their names on their cards.

3) Have participants stand in a circle and repeat together the words

on their cards, as a kind of pledge to be more childlike and playful in their daily lives.

4) Suggest that participants keep their cards in their wallets or purses, so that they are often reminded of their lifetime membership in the Society of Childlike Grown-ups.

VARIATIONS

- With large groups you may want to project the **Official Membership Card** as an overhead transparency, have people read it together, and then pick up their individual cards as they leave the workshop.

- You might want to print out the cards at a larger than normal business-card size to emphasize the fact that this is a most unique membership card with very special privileges.

NOTES

- Even though the **Official Membership Card** is a special reminder of the laughter and play participants experienced at a workshop together, have extra cards available for them to take home and give to their family members, colleagues, and friends.

OFFICIAL MEMBERSHIP CARD

_____

is a lifetime member in good standing in

❦The Society of Childlike Grown-ups ❦

and is hereby encouraged to express any and all
childlike qualities whenever, wherever, and with
whomsoever the member pleases.

© BRUCE WILLIAMSON

OFFICIAL MEMBERSHIP CARD

_____

is a lifetime member in good standing in

❦The Society of Childlike Grown-ups❦

and is hereby encouraged to express any and all
childlike qualities whenever, wherever, and with
whomsoever the member pleases.

© BRUCE WILLIAMSON

OFFICIAL MEMBERSHIP CARD

_____

is a lifetime member in good standing in

❦ The Society of Childlike Grown-ups ❦

and is hereby encouraged to express any and all
childlike qualities whenever, wherever, and with
whomsoever the member pleases.

© BRUCE WILLIAMSON

OFFICIAL MEMBERSHIP CARD

_____

is a lifetime member in good standing in

❦ The Society of Childlike Grown-ups ❦

and is hereby encouraged to express any and all
childlike qualities whenever, wherever, and with
whomsoever the member pleases.

© BRUCE WILLIAMSON

39 SQUISHER

Participants use balloons, sand, and colored markers to playfully create a physical object they can take with them as a reminder of the need to honor the child within.

GOAL

To create and take home a squeezable object as a reminder of the need to stay playful and childlike.

GROUP SIZE

Unlimited

TIME FRAME

10–15 minutes

MATERIALS NEEDED

One high-quality 11 inch latex balloon per person; some clean, dry, very fine playground sand (about ⅓ cup per balloon); scoops and funnels; various colored permanent markers or paint pens; tarp or cheap plastic drop cloth (for spills).

PROCESSS

1) Give each participant a balloon and then ask them to spend a few minutes decorating their balloons in ways that remind them to laugh and play more often. For example, they could write the word *MOOMBA* on their balloons, which means "let's get together and have some fun."

2) Have people fill their balloons with enough sand so that the balloon is completely full but not stretched out beyond its deflated size.

VARIATIONS

- Use larger 15 inch or 16 inch latex balloons to make bigger Squishers. These balloons take about 1 cup of sand per balloon to fill.

NOTES

- Although salt or sugar could be substituted for sand, the playground sand is by far the cheapest substance per pound. It's available in 50-pound sacks at most lumber yards and hardware stores for only a few dollars.

- Since 1 cup of playground sand weighs approximately 12 ounces, you can get approximately 66 cups of sand from one 50-pound bag.

- Paint pens, although more expensive, tend to work better on balloons than ordinary permanent markers.

- It's important to use good-quality latex balloons, available in bulk at reasonable prices from balloon wholesalers. Cheap balloons tear easily.

- Squishers make such good gifts because they can be squeezed into so many different shapes. They can even be thrown quite hard onto the floor, flattening them without damage while serving as a playful and physical way to relieve stress.

40   THE LAUGHING PLACE

Using crayons and markers, participants draw pictures that show what it takes to create a place where laughter and play are found and experienced more often, both on and off the job.

GOALS

To draw pictures of places and things that stimulate laughter, humor, and play.

To rediscover the pleasure and magic of drawing.

GROUP SIZE

Unlimited

TIME FRAME

10–15 minutes

MATERIALS NEEDED

A generous supply of different-colored crayons; one piece of white paper per person.

PROCESS

1) Have each person draw a picture of a "laughing place," an environment that stimulates large amounts of humor, laughter, and playfulness. Participants often fill their laughing places with toys, books, tapes, posters, cartoons, food, people, and animals.

2) If they wish, have participants share their drawings with each other in small groups.

3) Recommend that participants put their drawings on their refrigerator doors (just as they might do with children's drawings) to remind them of what their laughing place looks like.

VARIATIONS

- Have small groups of 5–6 people draw a picture together.

- Have people specifically focus on what a laughing place might look like at work.

- Have participants focus on the crayons themselves—smelling them, feeling them. Ask participants what memories and associations these smells and textures bring back.

- Have each person take home a crayon, as a creative symbol of the truth that it is always OK to color outside the lines.

NOTES

- Next to the people who think they can't sing are the people who believe they can't draw. Many people were shamed during their schooling into thinking they had to "color inside the lines" or told that their artistic perceptions of the world were "wrong." This activity can help people have fun expressing their feelings and ideas in color, without worrying about someone else judging their drawing ability.

RESOURCES

Crayola® crayons. For fascinating information about the history and manufacture of the most popular brand of crayons, call Binney & Smith at 800/CRAYOLA and ask for an information packet. Contact Think Big at 800/487-4244 for information about ordering five-foot-tall plastic replicas of Crayola® crayons. Discount stores also have less expensive crayon banks in various colors and sizes to use as props.

Drawing on the Right Side of the Brain. Betty Edwards.

Drawing with Children—A Creative Teaching and Learning Method that Works for Adults, Too. Mona Brookes.

Lighten Up: Survival Skills for People Under Pressure. C. W. Metcalf and Roma Felible.

Make Beliefs: A Way to Fool Around and Explore New Possibilities (You Can Write, Draw and Color Them). Bill Zimmerman. Drawings by Tom Bloom. At last, a coloring book for childlike grown-ups! Available from: Guarionex Press Ltd., 201 West 77 Street, New York, NY 10024. 212/724-5259.

The Light Touch: How to Use Humor for Business Success. Malcolm Kushner.

© 1993 Whole Person Associates   210 W Michigan   Duluth MN 55802-1908   (218) 727-0500

OTHER PLAYFUL RESOURCES

> Keep on the lookout for novel and interesting
> ideas that others have used successfully. Your
> idea has to be original only in its adaptation to
> the problem you're currently working on.
>
> **Thomas Edison**

LAUGHTER AND PLAY

Anguished English: An Anthology of Accidental Assaults Upon Our Language. Richard Lederer.

Calvin and Hobbes. Bill Watterson. These daily cartoons (and collections) tell the ongoing story of Calvin and his pet tiger Hobbes. It's certainly one of the best ways on the planet to stay in touch with the rambunctious, creative spirit of children—including the small child inside each person—and also to keep your laugh muscles well-exercised.

Flying Apparatus Catalog. This catalog, which contains Klutz Press publications and other playful items, is such an essential resource I had to list it again. Free from: Klutz Press, 2121 Staunton Court, Palo Alto, CA 94306. 415/424-0739.

Free Play: The Power of Improvisation in Life and the Arts. Stephen Nachmanovitch.

Laughing Matters. Joel Goodman, Editor and Punster-In-Chief. For current subscription and other information call The Humor Project at 518/587-8770 and ask for their free *HUMOResources Catalog.*

Laughter Works Warehouse Catalog. For a copy call Laughter Works Publications at 800/626-LAFF.

Pot Shots®. Books of Brilliant Thoughts®. Ashleigh Brilliant. For publication and catalog information contact: Ashleigh Brilliant, 117 West Valerio Street, Santa Barbara, CA 93101.

The Healing Power of Humor. Allen Klein.

The Whole Mirth Catalog. A mail order store filled with a wonderful variety of humor, laughter and play resources. For a free copy, contact: Whole Mirth Catalog, 1034 Page Street, San Francisco, CA 94117.

MUSICAL SUGGESTIONS

Using different kinds of music can help set a variety of creative moods in any workshop, ranging from relaxed to highly energetic. Many of the titles listed below can be ordered as tapes or CDs from the *Heartbeats Catalog.* Call Backroads Distributors at 800/825-4848 and ask for a free copy.

Relaxing and Creative

Desert Vision. Lanz and Speer.

Earth Spirit. Carlos Nikai.

Golden Voyage, Vol. 1. Bearns and Dexter.

Land of Enchantment. Deuter.

Piano Whispers. Charlie Thweatt.

Soaring. Tom Barabas and Dean Evenson.

Winter into Spring. George Winston.

Playful and Sprightly

Angel's Draught. Carrie Crompton.

Deep Breakfast. Ray Lynch.

© 1993 Whole Person Associates 210 W Michigan Duluth MN 55802-1908 (218) 727-0500

No Blue Thing. Ray Lynch.

Opera Sauvage. Vangelis.

Screamers (Circus Music).

The Music of Turlough O'Carolan. Patrick Ball.

High Energy

2000. Cusco.

Apurimac. Cusco.

Mystic Island. Cusco.

Out of Silence. Yanni.

Stars and Stripes Forever. John Philip Sousa.